MARITAL

MARITAL THERAPY
An Inside View

CHRISTOPHER F CLULOW
in collaboration with Lynne Cudmore

ABERDEEN UNIVERSITY PRESS

First published 1985
Aberdeen University Press
A member of the Pergamon Group

© The Tavistock Institute of Medical
Psychology, London, 1985

British Library Cataloguing in Publication Data

Clulow, Christopher
  Marital therapy: an inside view
  1. Marriage counseling 2. Marital psychotherapy
  I. Title II. Cudmore, Lyne
  616.89′156   HQ10
  ISBN 0 08 032425 8
  ISBN 0 08 032426 6 Pbk

PRINTED IN GREAT BRITAIN
THE UNIVERSITY PRESS
ABERDEEN

Contents

. . . most of us fear the extremes of pleasure, joy and love far more than hate, anxiety and despair. The negative emotions close us in upon ourselves, tether us safely to the ground, help us to feel clearly defined. They are familiar, repetitive, known, while the most positive emotions encourage us to abandon ourselves and threaten change and growth, even perhaps surrender to others or to causes greater than our petty selves.

Robin Skynner
(from David Scharff's *The Sexual Relationship*)

CHAPTER 1

Marital Therapy in Context

The Greeks had a word for it: θερᾰπεία. Therapy. Commonly assumed to mean *curing*, or *healing*, its first meaning is *waiting on, serving, attending*. In a social and professional climate which demands answers to questions, solutions to problems, and remedies for all ills this is a timely interpretation. There is of course no answer, solution, or remedy to be applied to the process of living. On that basis some argue that people should be left to carry on with their own lives free of intrusions from outside. Yet in essence life consists of the sum total of our involvements with the physical environment we inhabit and the people with whom we share it. In the western world it can be claimed that we depend more upon our relationships to give meaning to life than we do upon food and shelter. It is not surprising, therefore, that when our everyday involvements run into difficulties, we may need a particular kind of relationship to attend both to ourselves and to others who mean a lot to us. Therapy is one response to that need.

This book is about marital therapy—the process of attending to disturbance in the marriage relationship. It constitutes an inside view in three senses. In the first place it draws upon the personal experience of Diana and Paul Johnson, pseudonyms for a couple who came to the Institute of Marital Studies (IMS) for help with their marriage. Certain aspects of their relationship, those not generally accessible to outsiders, were highlighted during their course of marital therapy. They have consented to these, and to their experience of therapy as a whole, being used in this book. Moreover, they have read and commented upon the manuscript, directing our attention to areas of importance for them, as well as to errors, oversights and misreadings on our part.

While they feature prominently in what follows, this book is intended to be less about them than about Lynne Cudmore and myself who, as Mr and Mrs Johnson's therapists, attempted to make sense of their relationship with each other and with us. The book comprises an inside view in the sense that it is an account of the process of therapy by therapists. In

1

this account we have deliberately concentrated upon issues and questions which preoccupied us as therapists in order to articulate and underline our working assumptions and how they affected our practice. We have tried not to place the Johnsons too much in the limelight. However, we have relied heavily upon them to provide the crystal of experience around which our thoughts have clustered and grown. In some respects the result is bound to be a distortion, since we have imposed upon their reality our own. The Johnsons have endorsed the substance of what related to them as being important to an understanding of the inner workings of their marriage, although some differences over interpretation remain.

Finally, the conceptual basis of this account of therapy is psycho-dynamic. What happens in marriage and in the therapeutic relationship is understood not only in terms of factors which are observable and relate to the present day, but also in terms of influences and pressures which are unseen and often inaccessible to conscious reasoning, factors which derive from an inner core of experience, moulding, as well as moulded by interactions with what we commonly regard as the real world outside the psyche. Taking account of these inner realities and their manifestations in the environment constitutes a view from the inside.

The relationship between inner and outer realities, sometimes mutually supporting, sometimes discrepant, is of especial interest to the psycho-dynamically oriented marital therapist. The tensions between his percep-tions and hers, his interests and hers, are played out against (and often generated by) the changing backcloth of their relationship as a couple. That relationship also exists within a social context. To take account of the whole requires a capacity for seeing things from more than one point of view. It is beyond the scope and intention of this book to offer a comprehensive description and explanation of a marriage, but even the limited perspective of an inside view demands that account is taken of what is happening outside. Specific behaviour needs to be considered within the wider context in which it occurs. So it is that this account of a particular marital therapy attempts to relate to general therapeutic, theoretical and research issues in the hope that each might inform the others. It is also a justification for opening with a consideration of the social and professional context in which marital therapy is practised.

Marriage in the 1980s

It may well be that the changing relations between the sexes is the most significant aspect of recent western social development. If this is the case it is small wonder that the stability of marriage is more precarious now than at any time in living memory (excepting, perhaps, the years directly affected by two world wars). Marriage, *par excellence,* is where relations between men and women are worked out in practice.

Marriage is also concerned with balancing the need to conserve with pressure for change. Conflicting views about marriage are therefore to be expected. At the social level marriage has been blamed for oppressing women, causing physical and psychological ill-health, generating delinquency and inhibiting the development of wider community relationships. It has also been well-regarded for providing individuals with a role and social position, for fostering health through emotional security and perpetuating a sense of morality and civilisation. At a personal level most of us experience a similar ambivalence about marriage: it is the relationship from which we, at times, want to break out, and yet the one to which we are longingly drawn back.

Depending on your current view of marriage, statistics will suggest different images. The six-fold increase in the divorce rate over the past quarter century, the prediction that one in three marriages contracted today are likely to end in divorce and the fact that already one in eight children live in single-parent families (though not all as a result of their parents' divorce) inclines towards pessimism. Yet most young people in Britain today will marry, most married couples will have children and most of these will be legitimate and brought up by two parents. Moreover, most marriages (between two-thirds and three-quarters) are expected to survive as life-long partnerships.[1]

Those who conclude that marriage is at risk offer various explanations. For example, marriage has to serve the needs of individuals who live longer than before, are less supported by the extended family than their forbears, have more opportunities to meet other partners because of social and geographical mobility and are less tied by moral and social constraints than was the case a hundred years ago. They live in a culture where religious affiliations have grown weaker, one governed by materialist values which can suggest that relationships as well as objects may be disposable. Moreover, there are expectations of marriage to provide personal happiness and fulfillment, even to make up for less than fulfilling relationships in the past.

In socio-economic terms the most significant factor may be the accelerating participation of married women in paid employment, now freed from years of childbearing by effective contraception and afforded greater choice by opportunities to meet new partners at work (free of the confines of home and neighbourhood) and by reduced financial dependency on husbands. One review of divorce trends restricts its conclusions to three linked statements: married women are more likely to divorce if they work; the number of younger married women in paid employment rose sharply after 1968; younger married women are more likely to divorce than their older counterparts.[2] Add to the economic emancipation of women the financial provisions accruing from the Welfare State, the easing of divorce legislation and the availability of legal aid in civil proceedings, and it is tempting to describe the 'failure' of marriage as the redundancy of an ancient economic contract no longer justified by financial necessity.

One hundred years ago there were few divorces, but there is no evidence that marriages were happier or more fulfilling than today. The present high divorce rate can be understood in terms of our seeing what was previously obscured by a legislative veil, a veil which has been torn with the emergence of more egalitarian values concerning the relations between men and women. Yet people do not readily allow themselves to be caught up in the mainstream of wider social change. Responsibility for others, especially children, is weighed in the balance with self interest when deciding upon the future of a relationship,[3] and no-one gives up marriage without a sense, whether justified or not, of having failed personally.

In the face of change in marriage how does the marital therapist define his client? What is the 'marriage" to which he or she must attend? Once again, it is important to take account of perspectives adopted by others. Intervening to save a marriage, or to aid separation, will have implications and meanings which extend well beyond the confines of the counselling or consulting room.

For the lawyer, defining marriage is a relatively straightforward task. Marriage is a legal contract conferring certain rights and obligations on the parties, many of them concerning financial matters, property rights, and the legal status of children. A couple does not necessarily have to live together to satisfy the contract. In this legalistic sense marriage can be used as a means to legal ends; for example, it has provided a device for attaining citizenship or the right of residence in a country. In strictly legal terms dissolving a partnership requires no more than satisfying the conditions of the law (currently that a marriage has irretrievably broken down), ensuring the assets are redistributed in a just manner, and safeguarding the welfare of the principal dependents—namely children.

If you are a churchman the problem is more complicated. Marriage is then likely to be regarded as a spiritual union, sanctioned by God, the dissolution of which poses a challenge to spiritual and moral authority. In this context permanence and fidelity characterise marriage, as did once fertility; the edict to 'multiply and be fruitful' applies less today than in the past. While attitudes are changing, the problem facing the clergy at the present time about the conditions under which remarriage should be allowed in church reflects a view that marriage means first marriage, and second time round is second best.

The stability of marriage is close to the heart of politicians in their public life. Here there will be recognition that private freedoms involve public costs. Who is to pick up the social, emotional and financial price tag if two people decide to separate or divorce? The legal process of divorce alone costs the taxpayer about £40 million annually in legal aid bills. Approximately five times that amount is spent on children in care and more than ten times that figure is spent on supplementary benefits, the principal means of support for many of the one and a half million children brought up in one-parent families.[4] It has been estimated that if you add to these figures the indirect costs of time lost at work and the expense of maintaining medical, psychiatric and social services to respond to marital stress, the annual cost of marital breakdown is in the region of a billion pounds.[5]

These essentially practical and static views of what marriage is about may be reflected in the expectations of couples themselves. For some people getting married is an end in itself. With marriage comes a socially-conferred role and status. Miss or Ms become Mrs, although Mr remains the same. In these terms marriage is viewed as a social institution and expected to provide ready-made answers to some of the most important questions in life: 'Who am I?' 'How should I behave?' 'Where do I find my niche in the community?' When marriage is viewed as the destination rather than the point of departure there may be surprise and disquiet that 'his' marriage turns out to be rather different from 'hers',[6] and that both are subject to change.

Second marriages are very different from first marriages, especially when both partners have children from a previous relationship. Definitions of kin and family have to be thought out anew: how do step-children address step-parents? What authority have step-parents over step-children? How are the sexual or sibling tensions between step-relatives to be managed? Partners in a second marriage have to live with the implications of a previous marriage, to tolerate the commitment which encourages children to enjoy access to natural parents, to accept part of the household budget going to a former spouse, and to cope with the comparisons and evaluations which they and others may be making between 'then' and 'now'. Small wonder, perhaps, that second marriages are more prone to breakdown than first. The special circumstances of second marriage have social implications which therapists cannot discount.

The changes which are endemic in the family life cycle—including remarriage for a large number of families—require a dynamic, not a static, view of marriage. A couple's relationship will change as partners move from being newly-weds to becoming young parents,[7] from being parents of adolescent children to becoming a couple once more,[8] with many and varied stages in between. Each stage constitutes a turning point for the couple and for the partners as individuals, requiring a reappraisal of self and others, as well as a reappraisal of self by others. This is as true of predictable events as it is of the unexpected, like serious illness, bereavement or redundancy. Turning points, life crises of this kind, are stressful, involving a letting go of some aspects of the past and an adaptation to the challenge of the new. Events may have unpredicted consequences. The high expectations which accompany honeymoons (they still occur despite the growing trend for people to sleep and live together before marriage) may be let down by experience; becoming a parent may be a more taxing process than commonly anticipated; the death of a spouse can summon as well as drain personal resources.

Events which occur through the family life cycle have personal as well as social significance. In this respect marriage is a psychologically dynamic relationship in which there is a continuous process of integrating and reintegrating current experience in the light of what has gone before. As a psychological relationship, marriage is the direct heir to close childhood attachments. Conflicts in marriage can, in part, be understood in terms of old family scores being settled in current family partnerships. The nature and quality of the attachments we develop during childhood will influence the nature and quality of relationships we form in adulthood. We are, in part, shaped by our interpersonal experience, and once our expectations about how others behave are formed, we actively encourage their behaviour to conform with these conscious and unconscious expectations—no matter how damaging the consequences may be. From this perspective there is wisdom in pausing before discarding conflict-ridden partnerships, because conflict may contain the seeds of shared internal preoccupations which require an environment suited to their expression. Once expressed, marriage has potential for nurturing the personal and social development of adults as well as children.

This view of marriage as a vehicle for personal and social development is an identifying feature of the work of the Institute of Marital Studies.[9] It is developed in the pages which follow. Therapy does not address itself to the question of whether a couple should be helped to stay together or to separate, but is an enterprise which seeks to highlight, understand and contain issues (some of which may be hidden from awareness) which fuel interpersonal conflict so that from an informed basis individuals increase their freedom to choose, and do not feel compelled either to act precipitately or to atrophy.

Marital Therapy in the 1980s

However circumscribed the marital therapist believes his activities to be, they have social and political implications which extend beyond the couple who come for help with a problem. Marriage is susceptible to pressures emanating from the community and work, and from the physical environment; urban and rural ways of living generate their own brands of pressure to which individuals will be more or less susceptible, and more or less likely to bring home into their marriage.

It is on this basis that some have called for social and political action, aiming to change environmental factors in order to ease marital stress. Increased child benefits, greater employment opportunities for women, paternity leave for men, all can be described as having therapeutic effects for some marriages by easing environmental pressures. They have argued that therapy which addresses couples in isolation from the wider socio-political context can be construed as encouraging people to accept and live within their environmental straitjackets, in rather the same way that religion was in times past construed as a means of curbing social unrest by providing an opiate for the masses. Therapy is then regarded as a tool of the establishment, a means of ensuring conformity and resisting the tide of social change.

Others criticise psychodynamic therapy because of the attention it pays to early family experiences. The argument runs that this kind of psycho-therapy has turned up a wealth of evidence to demonstrate the damaging effects that family life, as presently organised, has upon individuals. Yet instead of changing the current parameters of family living, instead of looking at alternatives to marriage and the family, therapists continue to work with the same old problems in the same old forum thereby guaranteeing that the sins of this generation will be visited upon the next. The problem for these critics has been to demonstrate a viable alternative to family life and to show that structural changes in the fabric of society will leave a less damaging endowment.

An analogous debate continues within therapeutic circles. The point of difference here, however, is about therapeutic method, not about the object of therapeutic attention. Broadly speaking there are two camps: those who make their approach from the outside in, and those who work from the inside out. The first group works on the premise that introducing a change on the outside, for example by manipulating environmental factors, will effectively help people to change in the way they view themselves and their world. The environment can be the family circle. Systemic family therapists may help a problematic member of a family by treating the family as a whole, changing alliances and patterns of interaction within the family in a way which makes the problem less necessary for the individual and for the family group. Behaviour therapists treat symptoms in the belief that their eradication will have sufficient impact on patients to make symptom-formation unnecessary in the future. Each has in common a belief that small changes can trigger large changes, although family therapists would pay more attention than their behaviourist colleagues to the homeostatic properties of social systems which militate against change.

The second group works on the premise that the way life is organised externally depends, in part, upon the psychic organisation of an individual, a marriage, or a family group. These separate or shared inner worlds are credited with power to compel particular kinds of behaviour or patterns of interaction. The underlying assumption is that inner psychological convictions, often of an unconscious nature, have to shift before changes can be made and underpinned in the way a person lives his or her life.

Both approaches acknowledge, to greater or lesser degrees, the existence of two worlds, two realities, which struggle to maintain coherence in their relationship with each other. There is the outer, visible world of 'reality'—what we see, the events we experience, the environment we inhabit. There is also an idiosyncratic inner world, derived from highly personalised interpretations of life which define our perspectives, how we experience events, and the environments we choose to inhabit. Put simply, the dilemma is this: if we live in dowdy surroundings is it because we are depressed and choose to express our feelings by failing to maintain our habitat? Or, is it our surroundings which depress us and create the kind of inertia that makes picking up a paint brush too much of an effort? For the therapist the dilemma is about whether to alleviate the depression by relating to the individual's mood or to his picking up a paint brush.

Most therapists whose conceptual model embraces inner and outer worlds would accept that the two are vitally related to each other, and that it is unnecessary to make an either/or kind of judgement when considering the efficacy of different styles of therapeutic approach. For the marital therapist, marriage is an especially interesting meeting point between inner and outer realities. It is within the intimacy of marriage that the inner realities of one partner meet, as an outer reality, the inner realities of the other. As a couple, both meet the outer realities of the wider social world when it impinges upon the privacy of family life. In both contexts marriage has a reality-testing function: to work well it must mediate discrepancies between what is and what is believed to be.

Given the diversity of patterns in marriage, who is to distinguish between what is and what is believed to be? Inexorably, the spotlight falls on the therapist. Concepts of inner and outer space are part of a therapeutic model and, as such, beg questions about the image of man created by the therapist through the kind of relationship he or she seeks to establish with the client. By what criteria can an individual, a family, an organisation, or a community be said to be healthy? What philosophy of care guides the efforts of those who seek to help the ailments and problems of others?

The IMS works on four broad premises when defining its therapeutic aims and philosophy of care. First, stress is an integral part of life; emotional health is best defined by a person's capacity to manage internal conflict and external stress. On this assumption health is not conceived of as a state of ease or absence of conflict, but is characterised by a capacity to experience fear as well as trust, pain as well as pleasure, doubt as well as certainty, frustration as well as satisfaction. Second, significant relationships, notably those within the family but including attachments between client and therapist, can be used to resurrect and sometimes perpetuate inflexible patterns of behaviour established in the past. They can also be used to change such patterns. Third, unconscious processes need to be taken into account when attempting to understand problems in relationships—including the relationship between therapist and client. Practitioners, while attempting to influence those who approach them, will also be influenced by them, sometimes without knowing it. Fourth, change takes time because it requires a re-ordering of perceptions of self and others. This task is not lightly undertaken since perceptual models guide us in all our relationships.

Therapy is understood as the endeavour to promote the development of people in their social environment, assisting them in managing the attendant conflicts and maximising areas in which they can exercise both personal responsibility and freedom of choice. Defined in these terms, caring aims to assist people to manage the stresses and strains of living in a way which enables them to participate in, and to enjoy life as fully as possible. In this respect therapy can be compared with good parenting:[10] it aims to encourage neither a regressive dependency, nor a precocious independence, but to facilitate the development of self as separately viable, autonomous, and accountable, yet capable of interdependence in relationships with others.

The vital interconnection between the well-being of individuals, families, communities and social institutions is worth stressing in a time of rapid social and technological change, when welfare has become associated with a non-productive, energy-sapping and expensive enterprise. Philosophies of care have outpaced these stereotyped images by developing beyond the first-aid approach, beyond a casualty orientation, to embrace the promotion of individual and community well-being as complementary activities, not mutually exclusive options.[11]

Despite the best of intentions, however, criticisms about the enervating effects of professional care are not always without foundation. There are pressures from the community, from practitioners, and from the consumers of services themselves, to resist taking on appropriate responsibilities in times of stress. One study of a social services department concluded that the most demanding of the agency's clients benefited, above all else, from a long-term, reliable relationship through which the stresses of living might be better understood and managed. Instead, they pressed for and received a service whose efforts were directed towards making short-term responses. While alleviating current crises (for staff and management as much as for clients) this response usually failed to provide the kind of help which might moderate future crises and bolster personal autonomy.[12]

These problems have been preceded and paralleled by developments in medicine, where the provision of increased resources has failed to stem the demand on doctors' time. A document commenting on the rapid increase in the prescription of psychotropic drugs as an example of a characteristic medical response to ailments (many of which are essentially psychological or social in character), put the dilemma in these terms:

> First, it is in many cases extremely hard to distinguish between symptoms caused by a genuinely physical and perhaps serious illness and the same symptoms primarily caused by, or at least perceived as a result of social and psychological factors. Second, under the influence of traditional medical attitudes the scales are tipped heavily in favour of a physical diagnosis rather than a psychiatric one. Third, the patients themselves often prefer a physical diagnosis.[13]

There is, then, pressure on practitioners, both from clients and from within themselves, to do something, to take responsibility for problems in a way which, against their intention, can result in the use of more professional time and underestimate, even undermine, the resources of clients. Action of this kind may have less to do with attending to the needs of those seeking help than with stemming an anticipated flood tide of demand; as it turns out, perhaps, a false economy? Add to this the pressure from a community as much alarmed by the cost and growth of services at a time when there has been no obvious corresponding decrease in social ills, as by cuts occasioned by economic decline, and the climate for nurturing effective therapeutic enterprise feels rather cool. Small wonder that, on a personal and social level, the road to the therapist's door is paved with doubt and misgiving.

CHAPTER 2

From Surgery to Specialist

The Triangle of Referral

Mr and Mrs Johnson were referred for marital therapy by their doctor. Each partner had consulted her over minor medical complaints before they brought their sexual problem to her attention. She wrote:

> This couple will probably have already contacted you to ask for application forms, at my suggestion, but I would like to support their application for some marital therapy.
>
> They are asking for help with their short and fairly fragile marriage—both agreeing that they have considerable individual problems—but it seems clear to me that it is appropriate to look at their problems in the context of their relationship.
>
> Their relationship dates back for 2½ years, and they have only been married for about half that time. Diana Johnson (41) is eight years older than Paul Johnson. Neither of them has lived with anyone for any length of time before. She talks about sexual difficulties and loss of libido; he feels that he is very insecure sexually and is easily rebuffed, and has spent years of celibacy between relationships and prior to meeting Diana.
>
> They both had a strong commitment to politics and met as members of a political party, but both have recently withdrawn although it was their life. Paul claims that their withdrawal is not because of lack of sympathy but because they both, individually, felt they were overcommitted in terms of energy.
>
> My impression is that they are very keen to do some work on themselves and on their marriage and would be a rewarding couple to work with.

The appointments secretary acknowledged the letter and said that application forms would be sent to the couple as soon as they were in touch. Nothing was heard for three weeks. The referrer was telephoned to confirm that the Johnsons were not expecting to be contacted before making their own approach. A further three weeks elapsed before Mr

Johnson telephoned for application forms. These were despatched and the referrer was informed.

Three months passed without further word. The appointments secretary then wrote to Mr and Mrs Johnson wondering whether they still had the matter under consideration or had decided they did not wish to proceed further at that stage. A letter was also written to the referrer informing her of this follow-up action. Two weeks later a letter came back from her:

> I think you will find that the Johnsons will now be contacting you. Mr Johnson came to me last week in a very weepy, depressed state, asking for individual help, but commenting that his marriage was better. However, after talking to him, my own assessment is that this is still best looked at as two people with individual problems, but in the context of their relationship.

Three days later the completed application forms were received with a letter from Mrs Johnson indicating their availability for an initial consultation. Within a month of having received the forms this consultation took place.

Three main features stand out from the referral. In the first place, it took Mr and Mrs Johnson very much longer to arrive at the IMS for an initial consultation (six months) than predictions from the original referring letter might have indicated. Second, an ambiguity was developing about whether individual or marital help was the more appropriate response to the couple's problems: the most recent information was that Mr Johnson was saying the marriage was better but he was worse. Third, it was their doctor who, throughout the process, retained a conviction that marital help was appropriate. By writing to the IMS she instigated a three-cornered relationship involving herself, the Johnsons, and a specialist marital agency—the whole comprising a triangle of referral. As with the formation of any new system of relationships each participant had to decide whether and how to become involved with the others. Managing these boundaries raised, and raises in any referral system, one vital question: in whose interests is this referral being made? All the participants have vested interests. Because this is so the boundaries between referrer, client and specialist can become 'points of maximum dishonesty'.[1] The perspectives of each therefore merit close examination. Readers who wish to by-pass the discussion which follows to continue the account of therapy should move on to the next chapter.

The Specialist's Perspective

The letter of referral from Mr and Mrs Johnson's doctor raised for the IMS a question as to whether help was being sought for problems which were primarily personal (each acknowledged individual difficulties pre-dating the marriage), social (each had recently withdrawn from an activity which had previously claimed much of their energy and evoked their strong commitment), or marital (sexual difficulties were mentioned).

For an agency specialising in marital work the first and most obvious question concerns whether the problem is in any sense a marital one. This may not be as simple to answer as might at first appear. A physical event like an illness, or a social event like unemployment, will have reper-cussions upon individual marriages. But can these repercussions be regarded as marital problems? Marriage is an open system fashioned not only by the attitudes, expectations and experiences of each partner but also by a socially defined context, subject to wider family, community and social influences. Not even sex is exempt from these influences. Strictly speaking, then, there may be no such thing as a marital problem, although problems will be articulated in the context of marriage. Perhaps it is better to ask whether or not there are grounds for believing that a couple's relationship provides an appropriate forum for considering the problem that one or other, or both, are facing in their lives. The question can then be considered in terms of whether the marriage is easing or aggravating the problem, and whether there is scope for helping the relationship to help the partners as individuals.

For the specialist agency the process of answering this question has procedural dimensions. Through the referral letter and application forms information is made available from which it is possible to arrive at a tentative preliminary assessment. At the IMS these assessments are made by an Intake Committee which meets weekly to consider new applica-tions. The Committee members note on whose initiative a referral is made (distinguishing between referred and self-referred couples), the degree of urgency or pressure behind the referral and the extent of any delay in the process (recording in each case to whom that can be attributed). By noting references to sexual and communication difficulties they attempt to gauge how appropriate an offer of marital therapy is likely to be. Given that the Institute offers only weekly sessions of one hour's duration they also attempt to assess how suited the agency is to a couple's needs. They note whether couples or partners have received help previously, and any practicalities which might affect attendance. Finally, the Committee registers its response to the referral along with the decision taken at that stage (which might, for example, be to consult further with the referrer).

These deliberations take place against a background in which the demand for an agency's services has to balance the supply of its resources. The Intake Committee has a gate-keeping role in this respect, monitoring the involvement of the agency with those outside. The way in which it manages the conflict between the external pressure to accept referrals and the internal pressure to resist them (when staff resources are stretched) defines the agency's boundary in respect of therapeutic services.

An agency can make it more or less difficult for people to gain access. The broader its primary function, the greater the range of people and problems which cross its threshold, the less protected will be those working within. If agency boundaries are too permeable, practitioners will employ protective devices: some functional, like specialisation, others dysfunctional, like administrative remoteness. Boundaries of some kind are essential to survival. For agencies offering a personal service the dilemma is knowing where to settle along a continuum which ranges from exclusive rigidity at one end (permitting no relationship with the outside world) to unchecked permeability at the other (where a relationship is not possible because of the absence of any differentiation).

It is debatable whether, and to what extent, procedures should be allowed to define agency boundaries. Although not intended for that purpose, the application forms used by the IMS have, for some, deterred their search for help. Mr and Mrs Johnson, at the end of their therapy, told us how difficult they had found it to commit their feelings to paper. It had been for them as if they were being asked to set in concrete something which they experienced as fluid and changing, and to erect a monument of reproach which might haunt their future relationship and be used against them. More specifically, the application forms had a personal significance: life had been experienced by each of them, to differing degrees, as a series of examinations. Here was yet one more test which had to be passed before anyone would offer help.

Despite these drawbacks intake procedures can, and usually do, detect applications which are clearly inappropriate—either in terms of the applicant's needs or the agency's resources. However, there is no substitute for face-to-face contact. That was to come with the Johnsons through the initial consultation; but what of their referrer, the person who seemed most clear that marital therapy was appropriate? From the agency's point of view it made a difference that she had referred other couples to the IMS and was known to be familiar with the kind of service the Johnsons might expect to receive. Her judgement that marital therapy was the treatment of choice was therefore trusted and given weight.

The Referrer's Perspective

One might argue that there is never a need for a third person to match-make between client and agency. After all, if a doctor has identified a problem which falls within the province of a marital agency, and a couple agree that their difficulties might usefully be considered there—indeed, wish for this to happen—what is to prevent their making a direct approach once they have obtained the address? On the other hand if they are not clear that their problem is to do with their marriage, despite their doctor's conviction that it is, and have serious misgivings about attending for therapy, is it really likely to be productive to proceed? These questions might be rephrased in this way: for whose benefit is a referral being made?

At a rational level most referrers will answer that it is in the interests of their clients or patients to be directed towards those who are most likely to be able to relieve their problems. Referral can be the most helpful offer a practitioner can make when a problem falls outside his or her area of competence. For doctors, it is in the best traditions of medicine to refer to specialists conditions which fall outside the scope of general practice. Moreover, to do so satisfies the helper's need both to be helpful and to demonstrate the resources at his disposal.

It is here that cracks begin to appear. A cautionary tale from the world of social work describes the situation in which a home help is called in by a social services department to help a beleaguered mother clean up her home. As the mother and home help talk together, the latter becomes increasingly worried by the intimate personal problems being disclosed to her. She suggests she ask the social worker to call. 'Don't do that', replies the mother, 'she'll only want to *do* something about it.'[2]

One of the hardest things is to sit and listen to anxiety-generating material without being propelled into action. The subtle emotional pressures which operate between clients and practitioners are capable of prompting unconsidered and precipitate action.[3] For the helping professions, clients with problems which won't go away can, at best, be wearisome; at worst, they can be frightening. Referral may be initiated in a spirit similar to that of the old Poor Law in which relief having been provided for a period there is the expectation, if not direction, that those still in need will move on. More commonly, referral may be a panic reaction to allay fear.[4] Very often it can happen that a referrer is sucked into a climate of anxiety which defines and channels the problem in an inflexible way. The anxiety needs to be contained (sometimes by taking action, sometimes by purposeful inactivity) in order to release both client and practitioner from being instruments of its expression and to allow for negotiation, rather than compulsion,,to dictate the next move.

Other pressures are also at work. While, for example, a doctor may not wish to hear too much about the private pain of a patient whom he knows well, and who may even be a friend, he may also be reluctant to let go of what both may consider to be a special and privileged relationship. Quite properly there will be reluctance to hand over to someone else, unless that someone is known to be competent. The goodwill extended by the referrer to the specialist agency may be a crucial factor in enabling a patient to cross that agency's threshold. A metaphor has been drawn from the world of economics to describe the relationship between doctor and patient as a 'mutual investment company'.[5] Goodwill is an important asset of the company, available to be transferred through referral to a specialist.

Equally, liabilities may be the subject of the referring transaction. A sense of failure on the part of the referrer may motivate a not always benign build up of the specialist as 'expert', in a way which ensures disappointment for the client when specialist help is eventually forthcoming. The half-hope that the 'expert' will fail, as the referrer feels he has failed may, as well as being an understandable human reaction, contain the seeds of an important unconscious communication running throughout the referral triangle. After all, the person most likely to feel a failure is the client. How galling for him (at one level) if someone else succeeds where he has failed. Referral in such circumstances can represent a manoeuvre to avoid a problem rather than to find the best available treatment. It can also confirm for clients that what they find unmanageable within themselves is also unmanageable to others: a very frightening message, and one which can reinforce already strong signals from a spouse or other member of the family.[6] The process in which members of a professional network are unconsciously cast in the roles of the referred family members, and literally act out these parts, has been described as 'system counter-transference'.[7]

The referral triangle is capable of conducting latent signals which may be of more significance than what is manifest between those involved. The way referrers and specialists act in relation to each other can be understood in various ways, but there are good therapeutic reasons for paying close attention to what is happening between them as an expression of unconscious phenomena relevant to the client's predica-

ment. There are good reasons also in that the unconscious at work need
not principally be that of the client:

> 'All referrals contain an unconscious message emanating from the referral
> source to the recipient of the referral. Referrals may be expressions of love,
> hate or ambivalence; they may be manifestations of rivalry and competition
> or defenses against these drives. Inevitably they reveal something about the
> psychodynamics of the referring party and his transference to the person to
> whom he is referring a prospective patient and to the prospective patient
> himself.'[8]

The human influences affecting referrals need not be hidden from awareness. Most practitioners will know from first hand about the possessive-
ness and competitiveness of the helping professions, the irrational sense
of hurt when a client divulges intimate information to one colleague and
not another, and the anxiety caused when one's work is exposed to the
scrutiny of others.[9]

There seemed little doubt in the mind of Mr and Mrs Johnson's
referrer that their marriage was an appropriate context for picking up the
issues which had been discussed with her. This certainty was conveyed by
her vouching for their motivation and recommending them to their
future therapists as 'a rewarding couple to work with'. Despite the
element of seduction contained in this phrase there was no pressure; the
opening sentence of her letter conveyed her conviction that the problem
was sufficiently owned by the Johnsons for them to have contacted the
IMS before she had.

The ambiguity about whether their problem was of an individual or
shared nature and the delay in the process of referral, were taken by us,
their prospective therapists, as indications of how anxious they were
about defining the problem in terms of their marriage. That they had
been thrown together following their withdrawal from politics might, we
thought, have been both a precipitating factor in consulting their doctor
and a reason for protecting their marriage; the fewer external outlets for
a couple, the greater the threat to security when marriage becomes
troubled.[10] Yet the referrer held on to her conviction about the marital
dimension of their problem and in a way which was not experienced by
us as coercive, or born of anxiety to offload them. We speculated that
conflict generated by the need to maintain separateness in a close and
committed relationship was particularly acute for Mr and Mrs Johnson.
The referral dynamic allowed the referrer to express the anxiety-
generating marital dimension of the problem while sufficient individual
symptoms were produced by the Johnsons to qualify them for help from

some source. With the benefit of hindsight we might have predicted that this dilemma was to constitute an essential part of their subsequent work in therapy.

The Client's Perspective

In the same way that it makes rational sense for a practitioner to refer patients whose presenting problems fall outside his or her area of competence, it makes rational sense for clients to accept the referral and follow it through. Rationally, no-one likes having problems and people will therefore do whatever is possible to alleviate them. Yet the facts appear to contradict reason. It is a consistent pattern in applications to the IMS that the majority of those who write or telephone for an appointment (directly, or indirectly through a referrer) withdraw before they are seen. Even Mr and Mrs Johnson hesitated before proceeding with their application. How is this to be understood?

It has already been intimated that the delay in the Johnsons' application was understood by us to reflect conflict about locating discomfort in their marriage. Ambivalence characterises every initiative which promises (or threatens) to bring about change. The devil that is known is sometimes preferred to the devil feared. Sufficient internal discomfort or external imperative is required for change to be contemplated. Even then, the drive may be directed towards restoring the past rather than toward exploring new ways of relating. Any change can be disturbing because it unsettles the sense of self, the core identity.[11] Referral is bound to evoke mixed feelings, and the ambivalence of wishing for relief and fearing the implications of re-defining problematic issues can be immobilising. For the client, referral is not the routine step that it may appear to the other two members in the triangle. Help may be needed from the referrer to enable the client either to pause, or to gather momentum. The specialist may be required to acknowledge the step taken by the client and to have patience with attacks of misgiving brought on by the move.

Agency procedures may account for reluctance in pursuing the approach for help. Reviewing their therapy with us Mr and Mrs Johnson emphasised this point:

> *Mr Johnson*: If anything you over-estimated our ambivalence about coming here, because of the length of time. There is an element in that, but I think there were other elements. The thing that I think you missed altogether was the real fear about simply filling in the application forms (Mrs Johnson

nodded here in agreement). This was a reality and not ambivalence. It's partly my personality and exams etc, but nevertheless a real thing over and above that.

The other thing was that the time was one of working something out with ourselves—because, in some ways at that point, our relationship seemed to be getting better—and there was a desire not to rock the boat. It was a time of working something out between the two of us rather than ambivalence.

Mrs Johnson: I, all along, felt strongly that it was an individual problem, and I wasn't convinced by the doctor. But I was willing to bow to her better judgement. So there was a resistance from that. The way that we both couched the application was in a way that made it an individual problem— well, not knowing, anyway.

While the approach may be made difficult for some by application procedures this is unlikely to account for all abandoned requests for help. People still withdraw when they are permitted to by-pass the application procedure and are offered an immediate appointment.[12] Moreover, other comparable agencies with different procedures have similar experiences.

For the self-referred, withdrawal before the initial consultation is, perhaps, more surprising than for those referred by a professional intermediary (although there is often an informal referrer in even the first group—a friend or a relative who has used or known of the service). It may be that, for some, the very act of applying for help can have sufficient repercussions on the marriage to begin a chain reaction, obviating the need for further help. For others, there will be fears about what they have started and where it might lead.

For most there will be the problem of how to communicate discomfort. People communicate their physical, social and psychological disease in a variety of languages. Whereas social work agencies are often called upon to respond to enacted, as opposed to spoken messages, patients who consult their doctor are likely to couch their communications in terms of illness. It is because of this diversity in language that a wide range of professions come into contact with marital and family stress. Not only social workers and doctors, but solicitors and personnel managers (to take just two examples) need to be alive to the influence of marriage and family stress upon the calls on their time. This reality has justified the 'many doors'[13] strategy for responding to marital and family problems.

The doctor's role and setting invite the assumption that the language of illness will govern what qualifies for attention. The belief that nobody can be blamed for being ill makes illness a particularly attractive language to those whose complaint is not strictly organic but who fear the consequences of expressing the source of their dis-ease in inter-personal terms. However, if the illness is not verifiable in medical terms, if the language remains unintelligible in its original form, some interpretation must be made for the symptoms to disappear. But some patients value their symptoms too much to give them up easily. A chronic medical condition may provide the only legitimate means of seeking attention for someone who prides himself on his self-sufficiency. The status of patient may, in itself, prove attractive to a person who feels dislocated in his or her relationships. For all, the translation of illness into another language (for example, the language of interpersonal relationships) involves change.

It is the change of status involved in accepting the translation of bodily symptoms into relational issues which can result in one or both partners to a marriage fiercely resisting this new dimension. The designated patient may carry the burden of the marriage and express concern or protest through physical or emotional ailments. For the 'well' partner this may seem preferable to a condition in which both are seen to have a part and for which both may require help. Directing the spotlight of professional attention towards a physical or emotional complaint in one partner may be very much less threatening to both than directing it towards a relationship which each sees as fundamental to their own security. Willingness to entertain the translation implied by a referral (when, of course, the translation is appropriate) is a sign that movement has already begun.

CHAPTER 3

Across the Threshold

The return of completed application forms inaugurates the next stage in the intake process: the initial consultation. For the therapists this consultation has the dual purpose of arriving at a diagnosis of the problem(s), and assessing how far the agency is suited to help. In marital therapy the object of attention is not the individual, but the relationship between two individuals. Together they are seen as constituting an entity which, while it is permeated by internal and external forces arising from the two individuals concerned and the social world in which they move, is nevertheless capable of maintaining recognisable characteristics of its own.

This fundamental assumption defines the therapeutic ground on which marital therapists take their stand. It establishes a perspective on events, confers meaning on behaviour and thereby provides a point of leverage for therapeutic interventions. For marital therapists, the mood or behaviour of either spouse will, in varying degrees, be understood as symptomatic of the state of the partnership. Therapists will be unwilling to view the depressed wife or errant husband as 'the patient' to be treated or reformed in the absence of their partner. Indeed, they are likely to be as intrigued by the designated patient's 'better half' as with the presenting problem. For them, the interesting question will be *how far does this behaviour or condition in some sense satisfy, or act purposively for the couple, and to what shared preoccupations does it draw attention*?

This is an unquestionably blinkered position to adopt, one which may well obscure other perspectives and contexts in arriving at an understanding of what is going on. Is it defensible? After all, individuals exist in their own right, not simply as extensions of, or complements to, their spouses; together or apart couples move in other social circles—at work and in their respective families and local communities. The nature of these contacts will affect mood and behaviour and may well be the source of much conflict in marriage. Because this is undoubtedly true, an

22

answer is required to the question of whether a diagnosis made in a partial, incomplete social context can ever be valid. What safeguards exist to protect couples from being persuaded they have marital problems when other pressures may be of more significance in contributing to tensions at home?

From the therapists' side it is assumed that those who bring their problems to the attention of an agency which has the word 'marriage' across its door have, to some degree, sensed for themselves the appropriateness of considering their problems in the context of their marriage. There is therefore an element of client choice, albeit not necessarily a free or even informed choice. The choice is tested at the consultation: initial assessments are a two-way process, involving a stock-taking for couples as well as for therapists. At this consultation a couple will meet their therapists, describe what they think is pertinent to their predicament and hear how the therapists comment on and think about issues which have been raised. They will sample what therapy at the agency is going to be like and, assuming there is no change between intake and treatment, gauge whether they can put up with their therapists. Ultimately, it is the couple who decide whether or not it is for them.

That does not, however, relieve the therapists of responsibility. They will need to take into account the reality that those who consult them may not have either the disposition to be questioning in their approach (particularly given the authority of an agency and the transferential factors which affect interactions between those who require and those who offer help) or the necessary knowledge with which to make an informed choice. Identifying whether or not there is a marital problem will, in any case, be of less importance than assessing how a couple manages that problem between them.

The concept of a 'marital problem' is, strictly speaking, a meaningless one. It artificially segregates marriage from the real world in which the parties move, denying the relevance of environment and pre-married experience upon the individuals concerned. Here lies a paradox: does not the marital therapist exist to help those with marital problems? If marital problems can be dispensed with can you not also dispense with marital therapists? There is a way out of this paradox. Marriage can be viewed as a forum in which opportunities become available for identifying and working at problems expressed therein but whose geneses may lie elsewhere. With this view the only condition that has to be satisfied before an offer of marital therapy is made is that sufficient consensus exists between those concerned as to the appropriateness of using that forum for managing the problem. One important implication follows: marriage does not have to be under threat for marital therapy to be helpful.

Whatever the aetiology of a problem, the marital therapist can be relied upon to keep the marital perspective alive in the deliberations of therapy. A logical consequence of regarding the marital relationship as an interactive system whose workings cannot be fully comprehended without taking into account the role played by both partners is to offer assessment and treatment interviews only to couples, not to spouses whose partners cannot or will not attend. This is the practice at the IMS. It may seem to be an unnecessarily restrictive practice, but it is intended to convey that bringing about change in marriage requires a degree of co-operation from both spouses, and not just in the one hour or so a week which therapy provides. And given the assumption that each partner's behaviour needs to be understood in the context of the marriage as a whole, it is wise to ask what the absent partner's absence represents for the attender, as well as the attending partner's attendance for the absentee. *Between them* they are at the same time willing and reluctant. Behind willingness may lie misgiving; behind reluctance a wish for help.

What's good for the goose may also be good for the gander. A distinctive feature of the IMS intake and therapeutic process is the assignation of two therapists to each couple. There is a logic to the argument that if individual therapists see their patients on a one to one basis, marital therapists should see their couples 'two to two'. While providing a service in this way is costly in terms of staff resources, the reasons for co-working are to do with therapeutic opportunities and not economy. At its most straightforward, two heads are better than one, and a partner can be invaluable in surviving stormy passages in therapy. Two therapists allow for partners to be attended to as individuals as well as a couple (sometimes through the use of single interviews), and the co-working relationship is available to pick up the emotional undertow which may not be accessible in the manifest content of an interview. The clients' marriage may unconsciously affect the co-working 'marriage' allowing for additional dimensions to become apparent in diagnosis and subsequent treatment. Insofar as therapy often represents a kind of parenting, two workers constitute a two-parent family model with all the advantages this has for the family as a whole. Couples can relate to differences in their therapists and observe their relationship with each other; they can unite or divide their 'parents' and learn from this about their own early representational models of family life.

Of the many possible reasons why we, as a pair of therapists, might have become Mr and Mrs Johnson's workers, the salient one in fact was that we were looking for a couple who would agree to their sessions being tape-recorded. Recording, we thought, would help us to think critically about the kind of service we were offering to couples, and to articulate some of the assumptions guiding our interventions. We made a bid for the first available case on the condition that we would see them only if they consented to being recorded. If they did not want to be recorded, provision was made for them to be seen by someone else.

The appointments secretary was not enthusiastic about this condition. She told us, rather severely, that a couple who had hesitated as long as the Johnsons before applying for help were unlikely to want to contend with the additional burden of being recorded. She wondered whether we wanted to drive them away altogether? Our resolve held. Mr and Mrs Johnson were offered an appointment and accepted the condition.

The Application

When an appointment was offered to the Johnsons we had two sources of information. The first was the referral letter and subsequent details about the time it had taken for them to apply. The second was the application forms, which contained their respective assessments of the problem. The application forms, although experienced by the Johnsons as impediments to therapy, are intended not only to provide the therapists with additional information, but also to set in motion between partners a process of evaluation and discussion on which subsequent therapy might hope to build.

From the fact sheet we learned that Mr Johnson was thirty-three and worked as a tradesman. His wife was forty-one and a secretary. They had been married two and a half years and had no children. Mrs Johnson disclosed that she had received psychotherapy for depression fifteen years previously.

In writing about the problem Mrs Johnson conveyed a degree of caution and reserve, implying that she was not the instigator of their application but was responding to someone else's initiative. She expressed some confusion about the nature of their difficulties:

> I don't exactly know what the problem is but there are some difficulties, personal problems, that upset our marital relations and I would like to seek some help. Consequently, I agreed with our doctor that it would be a good idea to contact IMS.

Her husband was more specific. In weighing up whether it was his or their problem he assumed a greater share of the responsibility:

> Both of us entered marriage with a lot of habits and outlooks that make for

conflict; however, we seemed to bottle up our differences until, when we finally did quarrel, these quarrels were bitter and very, very destructive.

All this finally came to a head after a holiday in September; we discussed separation and decided we needed each other too much. Our relationship has improved, we no longer feel like killing each other half the time, but my psychological state has deteriorated. I have been suffering from uncontrollable fits of anxiety, crying and sleeplessness. I just don't know if this is related to the marriage or purely a personal problem.

I am bound to say I had a lot of problems in my late teens, early twenties (shyness and sexual insecurity) and suddenly all these problems, that I thought I had solved, have come back with a vengeance.

The Interview

Because of the question about whether they experienced the balance of their problem as individual or marital, and so, for us, the question of whether it was best addressed in the context of their marriage or not, we opted to see Mr and Mrs Johnson together for their initial consultation. As there were two of us, we had the fall-back option of seeing them separately if it seemed appropriate to do so. Another factor which swayed us was that Mrs Johnson already had experience of individual therapy, albeit fifteen years ago, and we wished to gauge their response to framing their problem as a joint one, and to test their ability to work together on the issues they raised.

What follows is an account of the initial consultation from three perspectives. The first describes the manifest content of the interview, the words spoken, although presented in summarised form. This account is numbered to allow for subsequent cross-referencing. The second is a commentary upon the interview, including some of the feelings, hidden communications and themes which accompanied the words. Finally, there is our attempt, as therapists, to synthesise content and commentary into a diagnosis with consequent implications for treatment.

Content

1   Mr and Mrs Johnson were on time for their appointment. Mr Johnson was a stockily-built man with weathered face and tired puffy eyes set within an oval of thick hair and a strong beard. He was casually dressed in shirt, jumper and jeans. Mrs Johnson was of medium height and build, looking younger than her years. She had a shock of short, curly brown hair below which were large eyes framed by

gold-rimmed glasses. She was dressed in corduroy trousers and a matching check smock. She was alert, earnest and showed no hint of nervousness. After introductions, we explained the purpose of the consultation and our reasons for wanting to use a tape recorder. Mrs Johnson asked who would listen to the recordings and was told that it was for our use only; they would be heard by no-one else apart from a senior colleague who might act as a consultant to the work we were doing. With their agreement the tape was switched on and Mrs Cudmore invited them to tell us about their difficulties.

2 Before responding to this Mrs Johnson asked for more information about us: what was our professional background? How did we work? For how long might treatment be expected to last? These questions were answered as far as it was possible for us to do so. We made it clear that we had no set agenda for the meeting but would like to think with them about what *they* considered to be important concerning their difficulties.

3 Mrs Johnson said she did not find it easy either talking or writing about their problems. She had 'difficulty in remembering or, more accurately, difficulty remembering things I don't want to remember'. She thought her husband found it easier and passed the initiative to him.

4 Mr Johnson obliged, but said he, too, had postponed completing the application form. However, once he had started to write he found he had a number of things to say. He described their problem as 'cyclical'. At the moment they were close, but they had a 'tendency to cut off from one another' which for him was a major worry. This oscillation he linked with strong and conflicting passions. 'Our interaction is destructive', he declared, but added he could not understand why this was so. Nor could they discuss it. It would be easier, he thought, if they hated each other, but that was far from the case. In the end 'it boils down to a series of recriminations with both parties feeling in the right'. While they were all right at present, only two months previously he had been to his doctor in a very bad state, and it had been she who had finally persuaded them to come to the IMS. He added that there were sexual problems too, but, again, these were 'difficult to discuss since we take it so personally'.

5 This clear description of a pattern of relating and the reasons for it prompted Mr Clulow to ask Mrs Johnson whether her difficulty in writing and talking about the problem was in any way connected with her husband's clarity about what was wrong. If he knew so

clearly, perhaps it was difficult for her to be sure for herself? Mrs Johnson thought that was right. When she considered things from her own point of view she was less aware of the drawing apart her husband mentioned, but then she saw herself as a 'self-contained' person and so perhaps it worried her less. Referring to their sexual relationship she said her interest had dwindled fairly soon after their marriage began. She was torn between feeling that this happened to most married couples and an uneasiness that, perhaps, there was something wrong with her. Mrs Cudmore remarked that each sounded as if they felt blamed for their difficulties.

6   Mr Clulow asked when the change in their sexual relationship had occurred. Mr Johnson dated it to six months after they had started living together. At the time he remembered wondering whether his wife's disinterest was a kind of provocation; he thought she had expected him to 'kick her teeth in' for cooling towards him. As they became more settled together he found his own interest in sex waning. He wondered whether there was a link between feeling secure and sexually unenlivened. There were long periods in their relationship, he said, when they didn't say if they felt angry or resentful. Then, finally, things would 'blow up' between them. Their worst row, four months previously, had followed a strained summer holiday. They had reached the point of wondering whether it might not be best to separate. But then the relationship had improved.

7   Mr Clulow inverted Mr Johnson's speculation about security being linked with lack of sexual interest by asking whether sex was better when they did 'blow up' together. Mrs Johnson thought that was 'not the whole story'. She felt primarily to blame for the decline in sex because she had found it less and less interesting. She thought this made things worse because her husband would become more hesitant and withdrawn. Mr Johnson interjected to say that he'd thought the lack of sex emphasised his own insecurity. He had always been 'severely shy' of women and had got round this by drinking. He felt a failure if his wife didn't reach orgasm during lovemaking. On the rare occasions they had talked about this he thought the details had been dealt with in a clinical way, relatively safe from feelings. Mrs Johnson riposted that the problem was also partly hers. In some respects she felt out of touch with her body. An essentially passive person, she thought she did not 'activate things' to get what she wanted. She then wondered whether it might not be best for each of them to talk separately with one therapist.

8   Mr Clulow responded to her request obliquely by asking how much each knew of the other's feelings and experiences. Mrs Johnson again passed the initiative to her husband saying he was more open than she—he had to 'drag things out of her'. He responded to her in a kindly manner saying he felt 'a lot more sympathetic' towards her since, together, they had visited the boarding school she had attended as a child.

9   Mr Clulow remarked on the likely relevance to the problems they were describing of what had happened to each of them before they met, and gave them the option of saying more about these current difficulties or telling us about their backgrounds. They chose to relate their family histories.

10 In a flat, matter of fact voice, Mrs Johnson said her parents had married young and travelled widely. There were four children of which she was the youngest; the family had moved about in the wake of her father's career. She described her father as a 'patriarch', a successful Israeli businessman who admired Britain; a man who was radical for his time and culture in that he thought women should have the same educational and work opportunities as men. When she was seven years old he despatched the children and their mother to England, and she went to boarding school. Although she hadn't known at the time, her parents had decided to separate.

11 One incident remained with her from that journey. Her father had given her a handkerchief as a parting present. During the passage she lost it overboard. She recalled her dismay at the loss, and her conflicting feelings of wanting a crewman to rescue it for her and fearing the waters were full of sharks. She did not see her father for the next four years and said that by that time she had forgotten what he looked like. With her sister, she remained in a boarding school for seven years and saw little of either parent. She said her father had not encouraged her to see her mother because he did not think she was a fit parent, so she spent most school holidays in other homes or institutions.

12 Mrs Cudmore asked what she made of it. Mrs Johnson laughed, and said that while she did not consider her experience as normal, it was all right, since others had been 'in the same boat'. She had visited her mother occasionally but recalled having arguments with her and then regretting the visit. Her father, and her politically motivated brother, were the two members of the family to whom she felt most drawn.

13   Asked about his family, Mr Johnson described what it had been like for him to be the middle of three children with parents who were constantly fighting. His father's work took him away from home for long periods, but he remembered the humiliations he'd suffered as a child when father returned to the family. The picture he painted was of an ultra-macho figure, devoid of sensitivity, for whom 'crying was rated above rape as a crime'. This image of father was a vivid one, and Mr Johnson recognised how his feelings coloured his description.

14   His relationship with his mother, although closer, was cautious. She was an emotionally volatile woman who sometimes let him more into her life than was comfortable for him. Adolescence was punctuated by anxiety, attacks of asthma, feelings of uncontrollable panic and a fear that there was something radically wrong with him. He said he coped by allowing hectic activity to come between himself and his feelings, a condition he described as 'walking around with a red hot poker up my arse'. Recently he had suffered a resurgence of these symptoms, as if this was a time when 'old things have come out of the closet'.

15   Mrs Cudmore asked what had attracted them to each other. Mrs Johnson replied that she had reached a point in her life when she wanted to settle down; with Mr Johnson she felt comfortable and secure: 'I was able to be—and say—myself with him'. Physical attraction had been less important for her than it had been for him. He had met her when they were both active in an organisation noted for social and political protest. In his view Mrs Johnson had no difficulty saying unpopular things within that organisation, something he both admired and feared about her. They also had in common the experience of being on the rebound from other relationships. Perhaps uncharacteristically, Mrs Johnson had initiated the courtship, and within weeks Mr Johnson had moved into her flat. Recently they had resigned from the organisation which had formerly occupied such an important part of their joint lives.

16   After hearing their accounts, Mr Clulow said he thought they'd been prepared to take risks by getting married. Each had accumulated enough experience separately to urge caution in making relationships. He ventured to suggest that there was a kind of positive inevitability about the difficulties they were experiencing with each other. Having become attached they had exposed themselves to feelings and anxieties generated in earlier times and against which they

wished to protect themselves, but these were easily re-evoked by current stresses. Some of these feelings were connected with losses. Perhaps they were worried about relationships not surviving too much closeness? They agreed but did not pursue the idea.

17 Mrs Cudmore commented on the changes Mrs Johnson had gone through in her life and yet how little bothered she'd seemed when telling us about them. Mrs Johnson explained that her father had taken all the family decisions at that time—he was 'like the God-father—still is'. She had accepted what happened to her.

18 As the interview drew to a close we asked them what they had made of the session. Mrs Johnson said that, at first, she had wished to be seen on her own since they both found it difficult to talk to each other, but with us present the process had been easier. Mr Johnson said he liked the idea of meeting together but was still worried how much they might be laying problems at the door of their marriage which were chiefly their own. We shared the dilemma about how we should see them, but decided that since our primary objective was to help them to talk together, as well as with us, we should start work in joint sessions. We concluded by making them an offer and discussing practical considerations, including times of appointments and the level of fee to be charged per session.

Commentary

Interwoven with the spoken word, the issues which people discuss and the content of their exchanges, lie assumptions, nuances and processes which form a second, and sometimes hidden layer of communication. Paying attention only to what is said results in an incomplete account of what is going on. Other sources of information are then overlooked. The process of an interview will be affected by the style of the therapists as much as by the contributions of their clients. Too structured an intervention may preclude latent communications. Yet there will be questions to which therapists need answers before deciding upon of making an offer of therapy.

It will be apparent that our style of interviewing was very open-ended, providing few guidelines and little structure to assist the Johnsons in presenting their problem and its origins. There were two reasons for this. In the first place, the Johnsons were encouraged to tell their story in their own way. The manner of their presentation was as important as whatever they chose to say. Accounts accentuate certain features of the domestic landscape and conceal others. We, as their therapists, had to decide what weight to place on the content of the interview, whether matters talked about were of the essence, or whether they constituted a smokescreen concealing other, more pertinent issues. In both diagnostic and treatment interviews, the question is constantly *why is this person telling me about these things at this point in our relationship*. Therapists are not apart from the material, even if they listen dispassionately to what they are told. The material constitutes an invitation to enter a relationship, and they must choose in what manner to respond. In making judgements of this kind much will turn on how incidents are described, the degree of feeling associated with events, what the feeling conveys to the therapists and the responses it elicits from them.

One criticism of this open-ended approach is that certain types of information are needed to make an adequate assessment.[1] Since couples may not know what information is important, they may need guidance and direction to use the time well. It may be appropriate for them to be given a detailed examination, a 'psycho-social', in the same way that doctors give their patients 'medicals'. These considerations lie behind the approach of those who adopt a structured approach, and who may employ check-lists or have set questions to which answers are required.

However structured the approach, no therapist is likely to conduct an initial consultation as if he or she were administering a questionnaire. Questions are so often met by mere answers, with no inkling of the import to be attached to information which is obtained in that way. Therapists are more likely to incorporate a blend of styles. Behind our open-ended approach to the Johnsons was a framework of questions which we hoped would be answered by the way they chose to use the session. For example, as well as looking for personal and marital histories, we wanted to know what they saw as their main areas of difficulty, why they had been prompted to ask for help at the time they did, what they felt most strongly about and the areas in which they were most anxious and/or defended, how they related to each other and to us, what their hopes and fears of therapy were, as well as their responses to our interventions.

Despite the implicit structure, it is not uncommon for there to be no comprehensive picture of the marriage and family background in the therapist's mind at the end of the consultation. More urgent matters may have taken precedence. There is no point, for example, mining for family histories with reluctant clients. For them, the most pressing issue is what it means to have come for help with their marriage. To by-pass this issue would be to evade a current reality of considerable importance, one which in itself may provide clues to understanding some of the difficulties in a marriage.

The second reason for adopting a responsive style at the initial consultation is to give couples a taste of what therapy is like in the agency they have approached. This allows them to be better informed when deciding whether or not they want to continue with that agency, and allows the therapists to arrive at a tentative assessment of whether they will be able to use the kind of help on offer. By checking how an interview was experienced (see para 18), there is opportunity for feedback which can assist in joint planning of future moves. At the same time there are quite legitimate client enquiries which require answers if a framework is to be established which allows the process of testing to go on (see para 2). They can be difficult to handle when the therapist is attempting to combine an interpretative and information-giving role. For example, Mrs Johnson's question contained a challenge which was not in keeping with the acquiescence which characterised much of the initial assessment interview. Here was an anomaly that might have been interpreted had it occurred later.

Mr and Mrs Johnson had little difficulty using the open-ended format once they started. They gave a lucid account of the problem as it appeared to each of them (paras 3–5) and showed considerable insight into their difficulties. The therapists had difficulty reconciling their image of two thoughtful, articulate and considerate people with the fact that they were describing a problem about communicating together. Yet there was no denying the reality of their anxiety about what they might do to each other. Discussion of the sexual problem (para 7) led each to retreat into blaming themselves for what was wrong, and resulted in Mrs Johnson asking to be seen on her own. As we experienced it, their anxiety was managed by adopting a self-blaming response and attempting to establish more distance. This process is of diagnostic importance because it echoed what happened in the marriage.

How were we, as their therapists, to respond to Mrs Johnson's request? Were we to accede to it in the hope of lowering the level of tension, perhaps thereby gaining access to sensitive information? Or were we to refuse to bow to the weight of the couple's anxiety and sit tight, implying that we thought these feelings could be weathered in a therapeutic setting and need not be feared so much? The latter option was taken up but with the escape route (para 9) of going back in time. Predictably, perhaps, they chose to talk about history.

On this subject, both partners were more at ease. They gave vivid accounts of their families, which threw light on why they behaved cautiously with people to whom they were attached, or might be in danger of becoming attached. Mr Johnson described the turbulent feelings associated for him with being close; Mrs Johnson poignantly justified a similar caution about closeness in relationships when she described her experience of loss. In some respects, stricken by adversity as they both had been, they were natural soulmates, and there were indications that each one's story represented something important for the other. The wish co-existed with the fear. Mr Johnson pressed for closeness in the marriage, although closeness for him was associated with emotional turbulence. Mrs Johnson described herself as 'self-contained', yet being apart from others had been painful for her. Subsequent events taught us that these positions were interchangeable; Mr Johnson was as capable of warding off others as Mrs Johnson was of longing for intimacy. In psychological terms, it was helpful to view both partners and the positions they adopted as an interacting whole, communicating a shared conflict about negotiating a manageable distance in relationships, torn, as they were, between the dictates of need and the cautions of experience.

The detail of their descriptions offered gold for interpretative mining. What might the sharks symbolise (the sharks which made recovering a special relationship with father—represented by the handkerchief—too dangerous for her, and which enforced upon her a loss to which she could become romantically attached, leaving little room for relationships of the heart to flourish with other men?) (para 11). How were we to understand the incitement to fury Mr Johnson read into his wife's sexual coolness towards him, leaving him with a violent image of male sexuality which he had fought to repudiate in his father but now feared in himself? Was his fantasy that he could only penetrate by kicking her teeth in? Was that the forbidden nature of sexual impulse and activity for him, or was he (as indeed he saw himself) merely a receptacle for his wife's aggression, filled up by her aggressive impulses which she disowned in herself? (para 6). Surely the depths which lay beneath their difficulties about being in touch physically and emotionally might prove fathomable with such material?

Yet we sensed a danger in responding to this invitation; it could result in our joining them in thinking rather than feeling. Too easily might we become embroiled in psychological games, weaving intricate designs as a protection against deep-rooted feelings indicated by their words. Here was a technical dilemma which stayed with us during their therapy.

The words created their own impression. By the end of the session, we were convinced that it was right to make an offer, that couple and agency were well-matched and that, for better or worse, we could in some respects talk each other's language. So, the unusual step was taken of making an offer of treatment there and then, without allowing for the customary period for each side to 'sleep on it'.

However, the question of cost remained. Money is an emotive subject and costs can be interpreted at different levels. Can change be afforded? What priority is the marriage to be given in the household budget? When negotiating fees, the offer made to us discloses something of the client's disposition as well as his or her means. An offer is a statement of personal as well as financial resources. Underpayment may devalue therapist and client alike; overpayment may exaggerate respective importances. Some feel exploited, believing it wrong to charge those made vulnerable by personal distress for help to which they have a right. Some welcome the control that payment implies, resisting any notion of their dependence on others. The IMS, by implication, says, through its scale of charges, that nothing is for free, and that our livelihood is in an important sense dependent upon our clients. The therapeutic enterprise is an interdependent one.

Mr and Mrs Johnson chose to pay the economic rate for the service. They were in a position to do so and their offer can be understood in rational terms of matching means with costs. But they also gave us no financial grounds on which to turn them away had we chosen to be inflexible about charges.

Towards a Diagnosis and Treatment Plan

The unwitting application of pressure to be accepted, to 'pass the exam', as the Johnsons later described it (Mr Johnson told us he had expected to be told: 'You're a hopeless case . . . I suggest you look at the "flats vacant" list') found its counterpart in therapists who wanted their consent to record the interviews. By agreeing to be recorded, by their apparent openness, by their capacity to articulate, and by the degree of fit between what we wished to know and their readiness to oblige with the minimum of prompting, we had already begun to see them as 'good clients'. At the end of the consultation there was little doubt in our minds that if they wanted to come we would see them, and apparently no doubt in their minds that they had already started with us. Perhaps we had also picked up how anxious they would have been about waiting before finding out if we could make them an offer.

It was only after the consultation, when we had a chance to stand back and take stock of what had gone on, that some anomalies became apparent. Placing what we had been told alongside our direct experience of them as a couple provided the means of arriving at a diagnostic assessment.

In the first place, we were left asking why a couple who had taken so long in their application for help, suggesting they had misgivings about the whole enterprise, should have been as co-operative, anxious to be accepted and undemanding of us as they were? How was it that the 'shall we, shan't we?' debate about coming into treatment was truncated—even by-passed—when it had featured so prominently in the preceding six months?

With the benefit of hindsight we made the assumption that some of the dynamics of their interaction as a married pair were also operating between them and us. Specifically, their misgivings, questions, challenges, and disappointments were being suppressed behind a positive veil in order to ward off the discomfort associated with differences which, if expressed, might have raised anxiety about jeopardising the therapeutic 'marriage' with us. In short, the prevailing assumption in the relationship between couple and therapists was that if we weren't in some sense 'at one', the relationship would break. Had we been quicker we might have predicted from this that once they left us after the consultation their misgivings would return, with the consequence either that we should never see them again, or, if we did, that there would be a crisis associated with negative feelings in the course of treatment, either between the two of them or between them and us (and possibly both). This latter prediction would, in part, have been borne out by events.

Scratching the surface a little more, we discovered that we were more 'out of touch' than 'at one' with them. Apart from Mrs Johnson's straightforward questions at the beginning of the interview, very little was asked of us. They might well have talked together for the whole session without requiring us to interject had we not made our own entrances. Our comments were infrequent, and it was as if we were being invited to be spectators, important yet remote from the action. Our contributions were usually agreed with (although Mrs Johnson expressed more caution than her husband in this respect) but they were generally not followed up or developed. In some respects, the session had been like a pre-scripted drama which we were invited to view.

We thought about what this might mean in relation to the content of the interview. In her application form, Mrs Johnson had written about her difficulty in knowing and giving expression to her feelings. When she told us about her childhood experiences we felt moved by her, yet her delivery belied any such feelings in herself, and she went on to discount their importance for her present life. Perhaps her feelings about events had been satisfactorily resolved in the past? Perhaps they were locked behind a façade of toughness and detachment? We took the view that insofar as she described her experience as if it had happened to someone other than herself she was in a similar position to us: a spectator protected from painful experiences by living outside herself.

On the other hand, Mr Johnson's narrative was dramatic and vivid, relayed in a way which invited laughter and applause for the skill of an able raconteur. It was as if he were acting the intense feelings contained in his colourful vignettes of family life. At the end of the interview we might almost have asked 'what's the problem', except that we knew, at one level, we had been told very clearly. Our experience was of simultaneously being seduced and kept remote. In their relationship the pattern was repeated: they talked of animosity between them at one remove, and behaved together in an accommodating and considerate way. Later in the therapy he told us that he talked to mask his anxiety: he feared what others might say about him if he stopped. The object of his fear had earlier been depicted by him as a 'red hot poker'.

The key to their problem, in our view, lay in the way they managed the very strong feelings stirred up by intimate attachments. To expose a need was to risk the frustration of that need, with the attendant fury this might stir up. Far better, one might imagine the sage of the subconscious ruminating, to persuade someone else to do the asking. But suppose someone else did? Might that not then become an unbearable claim on limited resources? Perhaps one claim would lead to another, would never end, never be satisfied? Much better to draw apart, feel nothing, switch off at the first hint of excitement or anguish. These feelings are bigger than both of us, the logic runs, much wiser to shut down.

Yet the lack of conviction and ambivalence about the logic within this kind of rumination, common to many people, was expressed by the Johnsons through their marriage and through their search for help with their marriage. The hope that things might be different through the mediating offices of their relationship together, and with us, was in conflict with the caution urged by experience of relationships past.

In the light of these conflicting pressures, it is not hard to imagine why it took so long for the Johnsons to come for help with their marriage. The acknowledgement of a marital problem constituted a threat to a couple who were anxious about being together, and even more anxious about being apart. They were able to take the plunge, not at the moment of crisis (after their holiday) but when they felt close together. The ticket of admission had to be an ailment suffered by one partner and mediated by a referrer in order to contain the anxiety about damage to the marriage each feared might follow from exploring what was happening between them.

Having made a commitment to each other, and having crossed the threshold into another relationship which offered hope, it is not surprising that the counsel of caution reasserted itself. Towards us they acquiesced. Towards each other they turned their recriminations inwards. Mr Johnson's somatic complaints and near breakdown in the months preceding the consultation can be understood as the logical extremity of this process, a self-destructive retreat designed to protect an important but perceptibly fragile relationship. Yet the protest still begged to be heard. We speculated that through the organisation in which they met at the very beginning of their relationship there were opportunities for giving vent to strong feelings; the politics of protest did not endanger the marriage. When they withdrew because of differences of opinion with other members, they feared retribution from those who had previously been their friends in adversity. Now together, and on their own, they feared their feelings and differences might place the marriage itself in jeopardy.

In the light of these considerations it seemed to us that the most important objective of a therapeutic offer would be to provide an environment in which feelings and thoughts could be known about, owned and, where appropriate, shared, without suffering the feared catastrophe of a severed relationship—either in the marriage or with us. Our role would be to promote the kind of reflection and discussion which focused on how they actually were *now*, and to be alive to the meaning of digressions as an indication of the level of anxiety stirred up in the process. In particular, we planned to look at what was taking place in the sessions between the two of them, and between them and ourselves. That would provide a shared experience of which we all had first-hand knowledge. This focus was not intended to deny the vital interconnection between their pasts and the present, but to counter the familiar recounting of a fable (in the sense that there is a reconstructed element present in every account of the past) in order that through a safer experience in the present there might be some recovery of their proper pasts. As far as was possible, we hoped, in that sense, to avoid archaeological excavations which took us away from an interactional focus.

We opted to see them together, although we might have chosen to work separately. The reasons for this were several. Some were to do with our own preferences and some were related to our views about what was most appropriate for the Johnsons. To the extent that they seemed to be living, as it were, inside each other's skin, the decision to see them together commended itself; without one, the other would have been incomplete.[2] Yet more convincing for us was the need to provide them with an expressive forum, a therapeutic means of containing their differences and passions, and for each to have the experience of surviving this. A decision to see them separately after what they had told us might unwittingly have been taken as confirmation by us of the risks of facing things together; it might also have encouraged a flight into individual pathology as a means of protecting the marriage. While it is possible to put forward convincing reasons for separate sessions, we made the choice knowing that, either way, some opportunities would be gained and some would be lost. At that point in time our main concern was to test whether the difficulties they brought could properly be addressed in the context of their marriage. We wished to make it clear we would be attending to *that* relationship in preference to the psycho-pathology of either partner. The conceptual basis for our manner of attending is described next. Readers wishing to pursue the account of therapy should move on to Chapter Five.

CHAPTER 4

Room with a View

Marital therapy is essentially an offer of space to attend to a couple's relationship. The views, assumptions and expectations of each partner and each therapist will influence how what is said and observed is received and understood. The interplay of these assumptions defines the nature of the therapeutic relationship.

Mr and Mrs Johnson's therapy was informed by a psychodynamic conceptual framework. The purpose of this chapter is to draw together certain concepts into a coherent framework and so describe the vantage point from which we, as therapists, saw and made sense of what was said and observed in the course of our relationship with them. Our framework rested on three premises: first, symptoms have a value and serve a purpose; second, marriage is a psychosocial organism, an entity capable of being understood and related to in its own right; third, there is a relationship between marital conflict and personal development.

Symptom and Signpost

Afflicted by symptoms, we search for a cure. No doubt affected by the impressive advances in medical technology this century, the influence of medicine upon the way we think about health and ill-health has encouraged the view that cures always exist, and that they lie not in ourselves but in the hands of specialist others. As patients we submit ourselves passively to investigation and treatment—sometimes regressing to a state of infantile dependence—confident that specialists will know what is wrong with us and, more importantly, be able to put it right. Sometimes we behave as if we view ourselves like a faulty machine, believing once the offending part is repaired—increasingly, replaced—we shall once again be firing on all cylinders, ready to carry on in exactly the same way as before. In this frame of mind we seek to dispense with our symptoms rather than entertain the idea that they might be old allies.

Couples seeking help for their marriage are in a different position from patients approaching their doctor, yet some of the same assumptions may apply. Although in more considered moments they will recognise there is no *remedy* for life, and will adjust their expectations of therapy accordingly, the hope for a ready-made answer to marital problems will persist. The expectations that therapists will declare for or against a marriage and the parties to it, will dispense good advice, and will prescribe courses of action guaranteed to neutralise trouble spots in a relationship need addressing before a therapeutic alliance can be established. In short, there is pressure for someone else to take responsibility for a problem which is thought to exist 'out there' rather than 'in here'.

There are, of course, exceptions. Mr and Mrs Johnson appeared to have no such expectations in their first meeting; quite the reverse in fact. Their problem was described by them in a remarkably self-sufficient manner, requiring little in the way of leading or prompting and, seemingly, expecting little of us in terms of a response. Yet we understood later that this was not the whole story. Mr Johnson talked at a subsequent interview about having felt as if judgement were being passed on him and their marriage during the initial consultation when one of us had made a comment to the effect that by marrying they had been prepared to take risks. The weight attached to what we said implied that, at an unspoken level, expectations of us and fears about therapy were then running high.

The fear of placing their relationship in jeopardy, we believed, had affected the way their symptoms were defined and presented. There was a sexual problem, described in terms of Mrs Johnson's loss of interest in sex and her partner's sexual insecurity; and there was a personal problem, described in terms of Mr Johnson's depressive symptoms. The sexual definition placed them on dangerous ground. Because of the emotional lability of this terrain each tended to *say* that the problem was their own, or even to agree that it might be accounted for by Mr Johnson's emotional state, whereas it later turned out that each *felt* the problem was the fault of the other. What was *said* tended to conceal what was *felt*.

In the tradition of psychodynamic therapy we assumed their presenting complaints had a shared meaning and purpose. When our attention was drawn to Mrs Johnson's loss of libido, or Mr Johnson's depressive episodes, we were impressed by the isolating *effects* of the symptoms and wondered whether these served to protect as well as draw attention to each other's needs as individuals. As their attributes had been parcelled out between them, Mrs Johnson expressed a need for distance and privacy while Mr Johnson declared a wish to be close, registering his distress and protest at her remoteness. This teleological view, serving to underline the functional nature of the symptoms for the couple (drawing them into therapy yet at the same time expressing their caution about involvement with each other and with us on any basis that might threaten the marriage) made it impossible for us to disconnect their symptoms from their emotional make-up as individuals and from the nature of their relationship with each other. However distressing, we assumed the symptoms had a value for them both. A therapeutic aim for us was to elucidate the nature of that value (a process sometimes referred to as working with the defence) and not to discount it in our hurry to bring about change. For the Johnsons we surmised that the symptoms had a protective value: they protected each partner from knowing about or experiencing too much of their own needs and feelings because there were associated fears that their relationship would be unable to bear the burden. Acknowledging this, we thought, might be a necessary preliminary to the pursuit of greater intimacy in the marriage.

However, we have said that each partner *felt* as if the other were really to blame for the lack of satisfaction being experienced at that time. Mrs Johnson felt she had to protect herself from the bundle of needs, if not nerves, that she saw in the demanding and self-preoccupied behaviour of her husband. Mr Johnson felt at a loss about how to penetrate the wall of reserve and disinterest he perceived in his wife. In attempting to understand this state of affairs we also assumed that what each complained about in the other was, to some extent, what they were least able to tolerate in themselves. So, we assumed Mrs Johnson protected herself from her own neediness by relating to needs in her husband, and Mr Johnson protected himself from his caution and reserve by relating to his wife's withholding behaviour. The corollary was that neither felt responsible for what was happening to them, despite their verbal acknowledgement that it took six of one and half a dozen of the other to end up where they were.

An important aim of psychotherapy is to help people accept and live with responsibility for their situation, and to understand scapegoating as a means of dealing with internal discomfort. Redrawing the boundaries of marital conflict in a way which makes a connection between interpersonal tensions and the conflicts individuals have within themselves highlights an important, and, at first sight, contradictory statement about the place of interpersonal relationships in working out the major preoccupation in life: a person's relationship with self. The contradiction disappears when it becomes apparent that self-realisation depends upon others. Relationships within marriage and the family, at work, and in the wider social environment serve to express and to meet the need to feel at one with oneself, a need which, when satisfied, results in the experience of living an interdependent yet integrated and purposeful life. The Johnsons' presenting complaint signalled a frustration of that need and the wish to do something about it in the marriage.

Marriage as a Psychological System

A functional view of marital symptoms implies an interactional view of pathology. Not only did the presenting complaints signal distress in Mr and Mrs Johnson as individuals, they signalled a disturbance in the balance of their marriage and galvanised forces to restore that balance, to bring the system back into equilibrium. Loss of libido and emotional disturbance isolated the Johnsons from each other to such an extent that others were required to help in the stabilising process. However prone Mr Johnson was to becoming a psychiatric casualty in his own right, however poorly predisposed Mrs Johnson was to sexual arousal in her own right, the marital frame of reference enabled their predicament to be viewed as symptomatic of a shared pattern of relating, not as the problem of one or other party. The patient, or client, was the marriage.

When Mr Johnson assessed what was wrong in the marriage he was tempted to think that the problem was his wife's sexual withholding. When Mrs Johnson assessed what was wrong in the marriage she was tempted to see the problem as her husband's emotional intrusiveness. At the time of the initial consultation Mr Johnson would not have recognised himself as withholding in his behaviour, nor would Mrs Johnson have seen herself as demanding.

Later in the therapy such a reversal did, in fact, occur—Mrs Johnson wanting sex and her husband holding back. Viewing marriage as a psychological system allows such interchangeability to be understood as an expression of a dynamic central to the psychic life of the marriage. In this case the dynamic can be expressed as a needy self in relation to a withholding or frustrating other. The roles were reversible; the dynamic remained the same. The fact that the roles were reversible suggests that what was taking place between the couple (their inter-personal conflict) reflected an internal (intra-psychic) conflict common to each partner. This admittedly restricted and over-simplified analysis of their interaction can be represented diagrammatically:

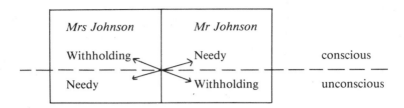

The Marital System

The intra-psychic conflict for each partner was between need satisfaction and self-protection. At the time they began therapy, Mr Johnson located and related to the part of himself which was withholding in his wife, and was blind to any reserve or caution in himself; Mrs Johnson located and related to the part of herself which was needy in the demanding attentions of her husband and was blind to the longing in herself. She protected herself by drawing apart, he protected himself by pressing in. This had the effect of further aggravating the polarisation in their relationship. This defensive process (unconsciously executed) which locates and relates to aspects of the self in another is known as projection.[1]

It will be apparent that the projections of each partner were, up to a point, accepted and therefore supported by the other. Mrs Johnson's tendency towards caution provided a home for Mr Johnson's reserve; her own needs and feelings were vicariously satisfied by Mr Johnson's emotional expressiveness. In that sense the marriage can be said to have constituted a shared defensive system. The concept of projective identification[2] takes account of the systemic properties implied by a reciprocal exchange of projections which serves not only to rid the self of certain properties, feelings or characteristics, but also to ensure that a relationship is maintained with them in another person. Projective identification has become an important concept in marital therapy precisely because it provides a bridge between individual and interpersonal psychology. It permits what goes on *between* people to be understood in terms of specific dynamic conflicts going on *within* them. For the conditions of projective identification to be met not only must there be a reciprocal exchange of projections but also there must be an active element in which one partner aims to evoke behaviour or feelings which have been repudiated from the self and is aided and abetted in this process by the other.[3] In short, there must be collusion to sustain mutual projections.[4]

Like all defensive operations, projective identification has a restorative as well as protective function. It constitutes a type of relatedness, one which blurs the boundary between self and others, preserving an internally endangered part of the self and permitting a relationship with that part to continue—albeit in another person. As such it constitutes a mode of communicating and opens up a pathway for psychological change. Through this mechanism, there is potential for integrating the fragmented self.

Against what anxiety is a shared defensive system erected? Why is a protective mechanism necessary at all? In Mr and Mrs Johnson's case we hypothesised that their needs, and feelings associated with frustration of those needs, constituted threats to the continuation of their marriage. These were the shared anxieties against which they attempted to afford each other protection. Experience had taught them it was dangerous to express their needs because others seemed unable to cope and either left (as in Mrs Johnson's case) or exploited their advantage (as in Mr Johnson's case). Expression of need risked frustration of need, and this, in turn, generated powerful negative feelings which tended either to be denied (Mrs Johnson) or turned in on the self (Mr Johnson) for fear they would endanger the future viability of the marriage. Their defensive arrangement involved collusion to present Mr Johnson, rather than the marriage, as the 'patient'. This suited Mrs Johnson's tendency to deal with her own needs and feelings by denial (loss of libido) and projection (relating to them in Mr Johnson). It suited Mr Johnson's wish to qualify for attention (through physical and emotional ailments) while protecting himself from the exploitation and exposure he feared would be attendant upon succeeding, fears he located in Mrs Johnson. It also suited their joint desire to maintain the marriage against the *shared phantasy*[5] that it would not survive the kind of separateness which permitted each to know about and express their different feelings and needs.

The marital system served to keep them in touch with their needs but operated a cut-off mechanism if they came too close. This was because needs and feelings were experienced as overwhelming, uncontrollable, and constituting a threat to the marriage. The problem was that this unconscious arrangement had passed the point where it worked benignly for the couple. The polarisation of their positions estranged the partners from themselves. Mrs Johnson felt she was denied her sexuality and Mr Johnson felt he was in danger of becoming a psychiatric casualty. As individuals they were laden and constricted by the extent of misattribution in the marriage. Paradoxically, the marriage came under threat from the defensive system itself. Here was the internal momentum for change.

One of the problems of examining psychological mechanisms in marriage is that it is easy to become blinkered and assume that marriage is defined and influenced solely by the partners and their interaction with each other. Marriage is an open system, affected by the couple's (and each individual's) relationship with the wider world. The marital system can be disturbed by events generated within the marriage (for example, the inability to have children, or an abortion[6]), and by events which impinge upon the marriage from outside (for example, the unemployment of one or other spouse[7]). Events of this kind have a social meaning. They also have a personal meaning which can enhance or diminish an individual's sense of self in relation to others, with consequent implications for marriage and family life. Marital therapists are therefore on the lookout for family and environmental triggers which may have prompted a disturbance in the marital system and provided the external momentum for change.

In the two or three years preceding the Johnsons' application for therapy two significant events had occurred. They had committed themselves to each other in marriage and they had broken their commitment with an organisation which had been demanding of their time and attention up to that point. It is possible to see the rearrangement of their external life as bringing home dynamic conflict in their personal life. For example, they had been drawn together in an organisation which provided a means of protesting against deprivation and exploitation in the world outside. As time went on, the organisation was itself experienced as exploitative, in terms of the demands it made and the uniformity of view it imposed on its members. These factors led the Johnsons to make the break in their affiliation. As a couple, they were then united in protesting against and separating themselves from the intrusiveness of an organisation which had begun to take on disliked characteristics of the world outside. Once they had left, they found themselves alone together, and discovered that similar conflicts were recurring between them. Yet their marriage was too important for them to deal with the problem by making the break from each other. Instead, they used their relationship as a forum to explore how these tensions could be managed in a different way.

Their purpose in seeking help, and the pressures on their marriage which caused them to do so at the time they did, can be understood in other ways. This is not intended, in any sense, to be a total explanation of their help-seeking history. It is, however, a way of looking at why couples come for help at the time they do.

Describing marriage as a psychological system buffeted by internal and external forces begs one vital question: what is the driving force which transcends the homeostatic, counterbalancing properties of defence and anxiety to allow for change? In answering this question a start has been made by considering the momentum for change built up inside and outside marriage. It needs pursuing within the context of a theory of personal development.

Conflict and Development

Throughout life human beings display, to greater or lesser extents, behaviour which is designed to restore their contact with a person, object, or even physical environment which, for them, represents security.[8] Attachment behaviour is exhibited most strongly and regularly in the first three years of life. Within three months of birth the infant has the means of developing an attachment to a specific figure, a process which in ordinary circumstances reaches its peak at approximately eighteen months of age. A stable and predictable environment allows the infant to begin to construct, in a way which establishes his trust and confidence, a working model of how others behave in relation to him and how he can influence their behaviour. An unstable environment, inaccessibility of parents (emotional or physical), or a particularly prolonged and unpredictable separation from a principal attachment figure frustrates this process. From a secure base it is possible to venture out and explore the unknown, to participate in life and to become involved with others without fearing disconnection from the centre, a centre which in adult life relies less upon tangible representation in the form of another person than during childhood. Nevertheless, at times of crisis significant others become especially important for adults too. When we are ill, afraid, bereft or isolated, we seek out whoever or whatever holds the key to our security.

Our experience of early attachments has a formative influence upon the kinds of working models we develop to guide us in subsequent relationships. These enable us to make predictions about how others will behave which may come in conflict with our need to be attached. The impairment of affectional bonds in childhood may result in clinging behaviour, in coercion, or in a certain detachment later on in life. These are all means of safeguarding against the pain of an anticipated separation from, or frustration by, important current figures in our life who are expected, on the basis of previous experience, not to be responsive or reliable.

John Bowlby's model of personality development draws on the biological sciences and uses a systemic frame of reference. Attachment behaviour is understood as a behavioural control system, activated by a range of stimuli, the purpose of which is to satisfy need or reduce fear by restoring proximity to a preferred individual. Psychological theories which presuppose sophisticated cognitive functioning amongst young children, or which offer explanations in terms of unconscious phantasy to the exclusion of recognising the validity of reactions to actual experience do not gain his ready acceptance.

Explaining the specificity of attachment behaviour in childhood and adulthood has puzzled and fascinated psychologists over the years. In Britain, a school of psychoanalytic thought has developed over the past forty or so years which has focused upon *disjunctions*[9] of experience resulting in inappropriate patterns of behaviour and response. At the root of the object-relations school of thought (the depersonalisation conveyed by the word 'object' intending to convey our capacity to relate only to parts of people and to inanimate objects) lies the assumption that the primary motive compelling human interaction is not the satisfaction of instinctual drives, important as food, sex and physical security are, but the need to be loved for oneself. During infancy the dependence of the very young child upon its attachment figure for physical and emotional nurture is almost total. Anything which threatens to rupture that relationship must be warded off, including the infant's own excited or enraged impulses and reactions within that relationship. At first the infant will have no capacity for recognising his part in the reactions of those around him. His capacity to differentiate between self and others will be very limited. When he feels good the world is good. When he feels bad the world is bad. He is the world; the world is a reflection of him. That good and bad can co-exist in the same person or relationship is beyond his grasp.

The seeds of conflict are sown later, when the infant experiences ambivalent feelings towards the same person and believes his own feelings constitute a threat to the relationship as a whole. To give an example, repeated withdrawal by a significant parent in the face of a child's temper tantrums may lead the child to surmise, rightly or wrongly, that it is his behaviour which drives the parent away. His outbursts are then thought to endanger the relationship most vital to his sense of well-being and security. For him there is a conflict between the need for security and the need for emotional expression. A means of dealing with that conflict is to split off from consciousness endangering patterns of relating (a process not consciously undertaken), repressing these patterns from that part of the self which is allowed direct expression in relationships. The angry toddler may become detached, ill or compliant in an attempt to safeguard his security. Later on, the child may attempt to manage conflict by relating to one parent as if he or she were all good, and to the other as if he or she were all bad. By working together the parents assist the child to integrate conflicting passions and perceptions; oedipal rivalries are survived. By separating, the parents may unwittingly confirm the child's belief (of which he may or may not be aware) that intense feelings have damaging consequences from which there is no recovery.

It is important to note that positive experiences and exciting feelings (libidinal relationships) are as prone to repression as negative experiences and feelings of frustration (anti-libidinal relationships.)[10] The image of self portrayed by the object-relations model is one of a matrix of intern-alised relationships, some of which are available for use in social transactions and others which are not because of the anxiety they engender. The more a person resorts to the psychic processes of splitting and repression, the more impoverished becomes his or her emotional and relational life.

Systems of repressed object relations were subsumed by Ezriel[11] under the term 'the avoided relationship' (avoided because of its association with 'catastrophe'—for example, separation from an attachment figure). Avoidance was not conceived as a conscious process, but one dictated by psychological defences. The relational equivalent of the defence was termed 'the required relationship'. The avoided relationship is held always to be seeking expression in the required relationship, resulting in anomalous signals and patterns of behaviour. These anomalies are the means by which it is possible to detect the operation of a defence.[12] They herald what Freud termed 'the return of the repressed'[13] and it is this feature of the model, the compulsion to repeat, which so closely links conflict with the process of personal and social development. Repressed systems of relationships cannot be forgotten about. Through dreams and fantasy they can find an outlet and stimulate creative endeavour. Throughout life they constantly seek expression in the ordinary discourse of everyday living. It is as if the self knows of its impoverishment and strives to reintegrate itself by demonstrating that anxiety generated by past experience is no longer justified in the present. If that demonstration succeeds, the self is released from a bondage of fear to participate more fully in relationships than before.

Repressed systems are particularly likely to find expression in those relationships most closely approximating early family ties.[14] Marriage is the nearest adult equivalent to the original parent-child relationship, endowing it with particular significance as a vehicle for personal develop-ment.[15] Although past anxieties may work unconsciously to demonstrate that nothing has changed in the intervening years, history does not *have* to repeat itself; the marital relationship has potential for conveying that liberating message.

All this may seem far removed from the problem Mr and Mrs Johnson were experiencing when they came for help with their marriage. At the initial consultation details of their history were incomplete, and although enlarged upon later in therapy, they remained so. It would, in any case, be a travesty to try and compress the richness of their life experiences into the confines of a theoretical framework. Yet theory can cast pools of illumination on otherwise perplexing problems.

From her vantage point as an adult, Mrs Johnson drew attention to the significance, for her, of being separated from a loved parent (her father) to attend boarding school in a foreign country If, as we surmised, father's memory was idealised and mother's unduly devalued (a form of splitting) this can be understood as a way of dealing with the mixture of pining, fear, and helpless fury that the event of separation was likely to have stirred up in a seven-year-old girl towards her parents. We do not know how over-determined the experience was, whether the event compounded previous experiences for her in which the world became an unpredictable place, but we do know that her parents used the separation as a means of ending their marriage, and that their decision was likely to have had an antecedent history which formed part of Mrs Johnson's environment as a small child.

The lesson she learned was to harness her expressions of love and be self-sufficient, only cautiously trusting herself to others. In this way she might avoid the rupture in important relationships to which she feared involvement would ultimately lead. Protest was expressed from a political platform, and a directness in personal relationships cautioned others to keep their distance. However, her private wish to be benignly enveloped by a close attachment was indicated at last by choosing a partner upon whom she could rely to express needs and feelings on her behalf. Yet the memory of a special closeness with her father, himself described as an enveloping figure, was preserved to keep her husband at bay. These anomalies draw attention to Mrs Johnson's wish for, yet avoidance of, relationships which placed her in the hands of others. Her fear can be related to the feelings which attachment stirred in her, prompting a determination not to let herself be taken over by them.

Mr Johnson's family experience did not centre upon an event of actual separation. The unpredictability in his life stemmed from being caught up in the drama of his parents' volatile marriage, privy to their secrets and vulnerable to their abuse. Attachment meant, for him, the forfeit of self. The rewards over-stimulated his passions yet frustrated his need to be loved for himself, conditions which thwarted development of confidence in himself as a separately viable person. For him, the required relationship was to be the entertainer, always available to others; the price of giving up this role, of differentiating himself from others, would be isolation from a system upon which he had come to depend for an ascribed identity, albeit one which could fluctuate unpredictably. For him, as for Mrs Johnson, the choice appeared to be between forfeiting himself or a loved partner. Differentiating himself, or asserting himself, felt akin to a violent act of assault and was therefore to be avoided. The fear found expression in reversed form. He once disclosed his fear that others might attack him if he allowed them too close; we believed he had attacked himself through his depressive symptoms. Either way, the knowledge he had to defend against was his own impulse to strike out against a world that would not attend to him.

Therapeutic Possibilities

While marriage can re-evoke earlier family experiences and encourage the reintegrative process of development, it does not have a monopoly in this respect. In varying degrees, all relationships hold out possibilities for self-discovery. Marriage is not necessarily the primary social vehicle for development and, as with other relationships, it may actually discourage the efforts of individuals to free themselves from the trappings of the past. Nevertheless it may be argued that within a marriage a person has the greatest support to change—and, if not, to remain trapped in the changeless repetition of past dissatisfactions. The nature of the bond is unique. It is unique in its intimacy or in the social expectation of intimacy. It is invested with an ambience in which to do its best or to do its worst.

Change is always a mixed blessing. No-one is anxious to amend or redraw the internal blueprints which, from hard-won experience, act as a guide to how others are likely to behave and how their behaviour can be interpreted in different situations. We not only learn from experience but actively work to make our social environment conform with our precon- ceptions. It is when we can no longer do this, when the discrepancy between expectations and experience creates a disjunction between inner and outer realities, that we are galvanised into changing ourselves, our environment, and perhaps both. The discrepancy indicates that our representational models are no longer compatible with the situation we find ourselves in and one or other requires modification.

Psychotherapy is a special relationship affording opportunities for change in that it aims to elucidate and to review the representational models, both conscious and unconscious, which individuals use to guide them in their social transactions. While remaining alive to the influence of social context upon behaviour, psychotherapy attempts to create the conditions in which an individual's representational models may become evident through the operation of transference (the transferral of past patterns of relating into the therapeutic relationship), and countertransference (the result of a reciprocal process and one which derives not only from the therapist's inner world but also from the roles unconsciously prescribed by the transference). Marital therapists make themselves accessible to couples with the same view, although they are likely to examine the manifestation of each partner's representational models primarily in the context of the marriage. One advantage of having two therapists is that transference and countertransference reactions have an additional effect upon the therapists' relationship with each other. In addition to the facility for attending to the individual in the marriage, shared working can allow the therapists to experience for themselves dilemmas which the partners in a marriage are contending with; in understanding and managing these the therapists may appreciate what is involved for their clients in making a change.

Change, viewed from the psychodynamic perspective, is essentially an integrative process, although one which may be preceded by testing the difference between self and others by a 'putting outside'. It involves withdrawal of projections and a capacity to live with oneself in oneself rather than in and through others. It involves movement from what Melanie Klein described as the 'paranoid schizoid position'[16] (where features of the self which are disliked or feared are disowned and ascribed to others) to the 'depressive position' (depressive in the sense of demonstrating a capacity to relinquish and tolerate the loss of defensive images of the world and to incorporate those facets previously projected into others). Venturing into new territory is easier when there is a base camp and opportunity for experimenting. Donald Winnicott, from his years of experience helping troubled children, described psychotherapy as concerned with encouraging an ability to play, itself a means of experimenting.[17] It is a vivid analogy.

Play is recreative in the true sense of the word, allowing for recovery and reworking of the past, and providing opportunities for imagination to break through the constraints of established realities. When the familiar is seen in a different light behaviour must alter accordingly. Play is best encouraged in a predictable environment. The Johnsons were offered two therapists, privacy and weekly appointments of an hour's duration—in short, a room with a view.

CHAPTER 5

Taking the Plunge

Diana and Paul Johnson were seen on thirty-eight occasions in the course of their one year therapy. What is reproduced here will be an unavoidably restricted account of the therapeutic process. Moreover, the wisdom of hindsight allows a clarity and form which was seldom experienced by us at the time we saw them, and the requirement of writing an accessible account has meant editing out some of the interesting and occasionally inconsistent byways which beckoned on the way. It was a therapy which did not depend upon interpretation of what was said, except insofar as that made the therapeutic structure safer and encouraged the Johnsons to be more emotionally courageous with each other. The process resembled less a journey, with an identifiable point of departure and arrival, than an experience, like taking a dip in the sea. The hope of coming out feeling more alive overcame discomfort from the cold and disquiet about being swept out of their depth.

Toe in the Water

Some say the nub of a problem is always expressed in the original contact with clients—in the diagnostic assessment. In contrast, the first treatment interview can be an anti-climax, a guarded and well-defended encounter after what is sometimes feared as too revealing an initial meeting. Yet the way any interview begins is worth attending to, since it may set the scene for that session. What follows is the transcript of the first few minutes of the Johnsons' first treatment interview. This took place two weeks after their initial consultation. Whilst their defences were up, they allowed us some insight into their way of managing potentially threatening encounters and in that sense defined their problem.

CC: Well, where would you like to begin after we . . . it was a fortnight ago we last met.

DJ: Yes. I don't know. I haven't thought of anything in particular. The only thing, you know, I thought of was . . . (laughs anxiously) I feel so nervous of coming here . . . how pressured I feel to think of things to actually have to bring up.

LC: Do you know what you feel nervous about?

DJ: (sighs)—No. It seems to be mainly not being able to think of anything in particular. I can't think of any particular problem that's arisen over the past two weeks, or, you know . . . I don't know, it might possibly be that I'm just nervous about exposure, you know? That's always quite a painful process too.

PJ: Yes. I thought a lot about our last discussion and discussed it with Diana to a certain extent. The most difficult thing, or question, that made me feel most insecure was the one when you (indicates *CC*) asked what we saw in each other. I'd never really asked Diana what really attracted me to her (sic) and I was quite taken aback in a way, and I felt a little insecure, in fact.

　　The idea of being safe and someone who could be relied upon, while that's nice, it's rather—I'm looking for a bit more than that. I suppose it's the romanticism, if that's the right word, you know what I'm getting at?—the passion, which I think is there but it's like we're really afraid to come to terms with it.

　　So, I know when we got back I told Diana I felt really insecure. (To her) I feel bad that this was the only reason you put forward. In fact, we had a talk about it and I felt a lot better about it; we made love for the first time in ages—well, quite a long time. But the thing was that after about two or three days I noticed us drifting into this routine where we lost contact with each other at a certain level—that's what I find. It's there, but we both of us tend to bury it and that's what needs to—that's the heart of the problem, I think. At the time I begin to feel cut off and isolated, and that makes me feel angry, and aggressive, and isolated. I don't know if I'm making myself clear? And it seems to go in cycles like that . . . we seem to communicate and then drift apart again. I find that very frustrating and difficult to handle.

CC: May I ask what you think it ought to be like? On the occasion you did talk that was fine, and then you drifted back into a sort of ordinary state. But I wonder if you've got a picture of how it ought to be together? What the relationship ought to be like to be a good relationship?

PJ: (cautiously) Yes. I think that it's not a question of what it ought to be because I'm aware of different things, different people have different things that they want. For myself, I need more intimacy. I'm not sure I like the word 'ought' because I have this idea of what stereotyped marriages should be like and it's not that. It's just something that I need, which I know is there, and very often we hit it off and can be very, very happy, but then it kind of drifts apart.

LC: Who drifts?

PJ: Sorry?

LC: Who drifts?

DJ: I think probably I do. I think there are periods when I tend to be very self-centred and in my own self somehow; and, you know, it doesn't seem to bother me not to make contact with things or with people around me. I go around in a kind of hazy (laughs)—I don't know what I'm particularly doing at that point.

I know that people do that in intensely creative moments, when they're focused on something, but it certainly isn't that. I just get set into kind of doing things that seem necessary to do, like house-keeping . . . succumbing to a certain kind of routine. Actually, my mind is just on moving from one step to another, really.

And I think my feeling about Paul is that he tends to need that contact all the time, you know? most of the time. And I'm not really even kind of conscious when I tend to drift in that way. The only time I can say it concretely happens is when I'm annoyed with Paul about something, like he hasn't done his share of the house-work, the washing up (laughs) or hasn't got around to *doing* some-thing. (To Paul) You go through periods when you're very lethargic, you can't bring yourself to do anything in that state of depression. So it's kind of a circular thing. I would tend to cut off and that would make him more depressed.

In this brief extract Mr and Mrs Johnson talk as if they are locked into a system of relating which expresses both a longing for intimacy in their marriage and yet a retreat from what, for them, are believed to be the burdensome implications of closeness. Mr Johnson acts as the spokes-man for intimacy, apparently unworried by any sense that closeness, romanticism and passion might also generate discomfort. At the same time he reacts against the word 'ought' when applied to his partnership, and differentiates himself from the imposition of a stereotype of marriage, suggesting an aversion and sensitivity to anything that might be experienced as a straitjacket. Mrs Johnson counterbalances him by remaining alive only to a need to protect herself (by 'drifting') from what she fears will turn out to be continuous claims on her if he comes too close.

Each partner makes an active (if unwitting) contribution towards sustaining this pattern—the 'routine' (his expression) or 'circular thing' (her description). Mr Johnson conveys his need through a depressive, self-engrossed appeal which gives a self-fulfilling aspect to his pessimistic expectations in that Mrs Johnson, in fact, withdraws in irritation. A safe distance is preserved. There are also hints that the roles might be interchangeable. Mrs Johnson's anger at her husband's self-enclosure (which she describes as his lethargy and depression) suggests not only that he is quite as capable of withdrawing as she, but also that she has hopes of his meeting her needs—emotional as well as practical.

Their defensive system is deployed: Mrs Johnson locates and relates to her need for closeness in her husband while Mr Johnson locates and relates to his need for distance in his wife. This shared unconscious manoeuvre serves to protect each from the longings and anxieties which they differently experience as unsettling. Paradoxically, the more rigidly employed the defence, the more inevitable (by virtue of the mutually frustrating nature of the unconscious agreement) that the longings and their accompanying legacies of feeling will be revived.

If the focus of attention is switched from their interaction as a couple to their interaction with their therapists and the idea of therapy, some similar patterns become evident. Commitment to therapy went hand in hand with a hope that things would improve in the marriage. Yet the desire for improvement carried hidden costs (for example, self-exposure, permeation of personal defences, disturbance of familiar patterns of relating) all of which were likely to give rise to misgivings and make the pursuit of change, quite appropriately, an ambivalent quest. The formal intimacy of therapy might be expected to exacerbate Mrs Johnson's caution and tendency to 'drift', given what she had said about the marriage. To formulate a problem might be to invite unwelcome attention to certain areas of the marriage and herself. Yet she had decided to engage in therapy—a process which entails acceptance of both the existence of a problem and the need for help from another. Evidence of her dilemma and her response to it can be read into her opening statements.

Whereas Mrs Johnson spoke to her need for self protection, and her sense of being 'pressured' by what she regarded as the expectations of the therapists, Mr Johnson seemed untroubled by a need for caution. Perhaps it is more accurate to say that his caution was directed not towards the prospect of intimacy, as was his wife's, but towards the threat of separateness and differentiation in the way they perceived their marriage. Because Mrs Johnson had placed more emphasis on security than passion in talking about her reason for choosing her husband, his view of himself as an emotionally involved person and of them as a normally passionate couple was challenged. The threat for him abated temporarily after they had talked together at home and made love (both good prognostic signs for therapy), but returned as their relationship once more became 'routine' and, in his eyes, distant. There was a point in the opening transcript at which he appeared not to hear Mrs Cudmore's question 'Who drifts?' At the time we had thought his apparent deafness to the question was evidence of his own self-contained style, which could be as upset by intrusion as that of his wife. He told us later that he had heard only too well, was anxious about accusing his wife of 'drifting', and so played for time. He was relieved when she let him off the hook.

With us it seemed that he (and they) wished to establish a fused relationship. Their language ('you know?') invited assent that we understood, while it also constituted a means of checking whether they were complying with our 'rules' so that they might pass what we subsequently learned felt to them like yet another exam. This cast light upon their anxiety about closeness: each feared being discovered to have insufficient emotional resources to satisfy the other. The anxiety was experienced at this point in relation to the therapists in terms of facing an exam which they had to pass.

In the context of the transference, the therapists had to ask themselves whether Mr Johnson's speedy involvement in the process of talking about himself and their marriage was altogether what it seemed, or whether it represented, at least in part, an attempt to establish a fused relationship with us in which differences, conflict and the consequent possibility of rejection might be avoided. That there were reasons for caution and mistrust in these early stages of the work became apparent much later on when they reviewed their therapy with us. To give one example: our request to tape the interviews was readily granted, but it had particular significance for Mr and Mrs Johnson in that the organisation they had recently left taped every meeting in order that no-one could deny what had been said. A healthy paranoia might reasonably have been stirred up by our request to tape the treatment interviews, but such feelings were not spoken about at the time it mattered.

From this opening theme a dynamic pattern can be detected which is concerned with managing physical and emotional distance to regulate the intensity of feeling associated with intimacy. This dynamic was repeated continually in the course of the thirty-eight sessions, sometimes accompanied by secondary themes and diversionary passages, always illustrated with rich, colourful and sometimes dramatic material. There was no sudden or radical improvement as a result of therapy; what we witnessed was a slow but steady process (sometimes punctuated by crisis) which enabled them to become less entangled in their 'dance routine'. Paradoxically, their greater ability to tolerate separateness in the marriage enabled them to become closer. But that was to come later.

The Shallows

Reading through the transcripts of the first seven meetings with the Johnsons brought back the elusiveness of our early experience of working with them. At one level it was as if the interviews opened up a limitless sea of material. In that sense the experience was overwhelming. A wealth of words, thoughts and memories permeated the interviews, allowing an unbounded stream of associations. It was as if we were caught in a strong tide and drawn hither and thither by the pulls of numerous undercurrents. The experience had its intoxicating moments, as when we listened to the Johnsons vividly describing their marriage, and reflected that every word was being recorded on the slow turning reels of our somewhat antiquated tape recorder.

But at another level it was as if we, and they, were paddling in the shallows, puzzled by how far away the water lapping at our ankles appeared to be. Then, far from being an asset, the tape became a burden. It recorded the extent and complexity of what was said in a way which was at times confusing and which defied comprehensive interpretation. It also failed to record the unspoken impact of the sessions—the sense of being at one remove from the material which we, and as it later turned out they, felt at the time.

The First Seven Interviews

The first treatment interview developed from its cautious beginnings into a discussion, indirectly pursued, about the cost of taking initiatives with each other and with us. Mr Johnson likened his state at home to being stuck in a car in the mud, spending time thinking about what should be done but never doing it. Mrs Johnson pursued the symbol of travel by describing her husband's fear of flying and inability to pass his driving test, which left her with the responsibility for transporting him. The reason for his inertia could be inferred when Mr Johnson recalled, with some despair, the comment made to him on qualifying by a tradesman who had seen him through his apprenticeship: 'Well, Paul, congratulations; but to me you'll always be a mate.' In other words, he felt doomed to fail.

At the second interview the difficulty in taking initiatives was taken up by Mrs Johnson in relation to us. After a half-hearted discussion about what was meant when Mr Johnson talked about needing 'passion' in their relationship, Mrs Johnson turned to us and described her discomfort at coming to the sessions. She said she found it difficult to focus on problems and felt bad about it—as if she'd failed to do her homework. She felt nervous about coming to the interviews and unable to find anything concrete to talk about. Mr Johnson put the problem in a nutshell when he said they were more concerned with what others thought about them than they were about what they wanted for themselves.

Mr Johnson talked later about how important it had been for him at that time to find out the unspoken 'rules' which governed the meetings so he would know how to frame his contributions to make him (and them as a couple) acceptable to us. In our view it was this constraint which inhibited work in the early sessions and confused us by giving the impression that headway was being made. They guessed they were expected to talk about problems in their relationship and to make connections with other social situations (particularly those in their families of origin) in a way which made matters more understandable. This they (and particularly Mr Johnson) did very competently. By doing so they complied with unspoken assumptions about the purpose of our meetings and it seemed as if we were being invited to share in a quest which had a common and therefore conflict-free objective. But the quest was, substantially, an intellectual one. It contained an emotional purpose (as understood in retrospect by us) which was to fuse us with them and ensure their acceptance for therapy. Our discomfort at being party to this was indicated by how little, relatively speaking, we said in the early interviews, and how difficult it was to find a separate point of entry into what was being discussed. Mrs Johnson's reluctance to speak, except about her reluctance, may well have been more work-orientated than many of the contributions made at that stage because it at least expressed her current experience.

Nevertheless, what was talked about was not unimportant. We were told that attempts to discuss sexual reserve had proved impossible at home and had not been pursued by Mr Johnson because his wife had once said 'if you don't like it, leave.' There were memories of half-hearted approaches made in the past, partly successful and partly restrained by fear of rejection. We learned that initiatives had been easier and sex better when lovemaking had been mechanical and the relationship less important. Now Mrs Johnson felt 'stifled' by her husband. She connected this feeling with her father, saying how important he had been and still was for her, despite living several thousand miles away and visited only infrequently—when she took the initiative. She feared she had never been loved by him for herself, only for what he had wanted her to be.

The mention of his father-in-law touched a raw nerve in Mr Johnson, who believed his wife married him as a gesture to please her father. We witnessed how her ambiguity about this fed his conviction. But it was clear that parental influence had also been present in *his* decision to marry. In part, his marriage had been a gesture of rebellion against an emotionally powerful mother, powerful enough for him not to tell her about the wedding. The significance of parents as figures with whom each partner was still preoccupied and concerned to establish appropriate distance and difference was well demonstrated.

In the next session Mr Johnson described how distraught his wife had been after the previous week's discussion. She agreed, and said she had felt pinned down and pressured by the interview. She had escaped to bed in tears when she got home. She didn't know why she had been so distraught but thought it was connected with talking about her father. We wondered whether we had been over-intrusive in the previous session but did not remember ourselves in that way. In what followed some anomalies became strikingly apparent: 'A good relationship means total exposure,' said Mr Johnson, going on to describe how he could fit all his worldly possessions into a bag so that he could be up and away at any time. 'I would like to be opened up,' said Mrs Johnson, after the tears which had been shed about people upsetting and putting pressure on her.

The fifth session was a threesome, Mr Clulow being away for that week. They talked about a row they had had at home. At the next session their appearance was very different: Mrs Johnson was wearing a dress instead of the trousers she had worn at previous interviews; Mr Johnson had cropped his beard in a way which gave his face more features. He commented that the previous week had been the first occasion on which they had talked in the sessions about a row which was still alive for them; he felt the week had gone much better as a result.

Much of this sixth session was spent discussing the false position in which they were in danger of putting themselves with us. Mr Johnson felt the 'raw edges' of his personality had been touched the previous week. He described how he talked continually in company to make himself the centre of attention yet also to conceal himself from others—to shut them out. He thought people might stop liking him if they saw through him to what was inside. The previous week had taught him two things: first, he might not be so bad after all; second he wasn't going to change fundamentally, and that coming to terms with who he was felt a better basis for going on.

In this and the seventh session Mrs Johnson also talked about the danger of being placed in a false position. She described her previous experience of psychotherapy where, she said, parallels were drawn with everything, and she knew what to say but could not *feel* anything. At home in the week they had been taking stock of their sessions with us. It was as if they had now run out of a script and were facing the rather frightening prospect of the sessions becoming unpredictable. As if to confirm this, we were told by Mr Johnson that he found himself drawing away from a wife he was beginning to find more 'pushy'. She had, in fact, recently made a sexual approach to him from which he had withdrawn. The tables had turned. This was less well-trodden territory.

In the course of these opening seven sessions there were several indications of engagement with therapy. In the first place we, as the Johnsons' therapists, moved from feeling we were observers at the sessions to being more enlivened and involved participants. Secondly, the subject matter of the sessions came closer to home. There was a shift from saying what might be thought 'appropriate' to exploring less acceptable feelings—those which impelled appearances to be kept up yet made for an uneasy facade. Thirdly, the locus of interaction became more immediate. From discussing what was taking place between them as simply a product of their separate family experiences, they were now risking and surviving expressions of difference at home. Finally, there were signs of change: Mrs Johnson was making approaches while Mr Johnson was beating the retreat. Both had risked becoming what they had originally complained of in each other and this suggested less rigidity in their projective system.

The Depths

Almost six months after they started therapy Mr and Mrs Johnson had a violent row. It took place during one weekend and Mr Johnson ended it by walking out, returning to his parents' home. We came to regard their next session with us, held two days later, as a turning point in the therapy. All that had gone before culminated in this episode which seemed to confirm the phantasy that their attempts to say what they felt, to be different from each other, and to become less entangled emotionally, were bound to end in the disaster of a broken marriage. This extract from the transcript of that session is dominated by Mrs Johnson, partly because Mr Johnson had been seen alone earlier that day at his own request, but also because she needed to talk before she could re-open the dialogue with her husband. At the time we saw them it felt very 'touch and go'.

DJ: (in a tense, low voice) I suppose Paul explained what happened?

CC: He told us what happened.

DJ: I don't know where to start. (Long pause) My feeling at the moment is that I am extremely alienated from him and I don't want to speak to him on any kind of one-to-one basis. The way I see things . . . I can't, I just can't deal with his insecurities which I think he transposes on me. I think last time I said that I found it difficult to open up because of his feelings of insecurity—in fact I think I said I thought he might leave if I did.

Paul called up a couple of days ago and said he wanted to contact you, and I told him this. His response was: 'I was expecting you'd had some kind of revelation, but it sounds to me just like the same old stuff; it's an easy way out for you'. That sort of confirmed for me that whatever possibility there might have been of talking to him at all was going to be very difficult. I felt like the doors were all closing—first I tried to destroy him, I tried to manipulate him . . . (lights a cigarette shakily).

LC: But you felt at the weekend when you actually did say what you felt, and you got in touch with things that really were quite bottled up, your worst fears were realised. He went.

DJ: Yes, and it seemed to me terribly easy to . . . (long pause). It's not the first time that this threat has been . . . the last time it occurred was abroad at Easter, when he just came out with it after a period of some tension . . . when I again had gone through a period of withdrawal because I felt constantly torn between having to choose between him and my family, and not being able to make any decision about it. And he forced me to make that decision—which in some ways I resent, actually, because I left that country feeling very distant and alienated from my father and his companion. The previous time I'd seen them I'd had much warmer feelings . . . but

I couldn't communicate with him (Paul). They (parents) felt *they* had done something, so when they 'phoned me it was a bit distressing for me.

LC: Mm.

CC: I think you both must have been very bruised by this weekend's events. It's not just that you are both very angry about what's happened, but you are also very hurt and in a sense much more vulnerable to each other than you have been, perhaps, for quite some time. And that's what makes it so painful and difficult about meeting together—wondering what to do with it, really, because part of your need must be to get yourselves together a bit after the eruption of the weekend, and feel you're back in one piece. And that might be particularly difficult to do when we're *all* here, after saying to each other quite demonstratively over the weekend that you needed to be apart—at least for a while—just to feel you are back in one piece. But at the same time, when we met with Paul earlier this afternoon we were both thinking this has actually been an important experience.

DJ: Yes. I think it's something that could be very positive. I mean, I don't feel I want to close off all possibilities. I mean I certainly feel very angry. One thing: I don't feel these things work only one way. I felt there was a need for me as well as Paul to express what I perceive in the relationship. I don't really understand what Paul wants. I really don't. I mean I could understand his wanting a closer relationship and there are clearly problems in establishing that. I certainly can't give that to him while I feel constantly bombarded by these insecurities of 'what are you thinking? What are you feeling? I know you resent me'. There doesn't seem to be any space to work that out. And I feel like he's trying to make me into his mother, you know?

CC: I suppose some of the space would come if you were less anxious about what you did to each other.

DJ: Yes. I just feel I need to relax a bit and I can't stand this emotional fraughtness, you know? and such a concern about 'the relationship' instead of just trying to 'be'.

A lot of the context of this is that Paul has just passed his exams and I've felt under enormous pressure. I've had to pursue my course, look for a job, and also sell my mother's house—and I have found it very difficult to cope. When Paul left it was just sort of easier. But another thing, when it happened—you know—that he decided to leave and bashed me—he insisted on calling up a friend because he thought I was going to 'go to pieces'—those were exactly his words. And I just didn't want anyone. The same thing happened when he said he was going to contact you to see if he could see you alone—he thought I ought to do the same thing and I didn't feel the need. All I felt was I wanted to come to the meeting we'd arranged, and I waited to have whatever was said out with Paul.

LC: Did you feel you were able to say at the weekend that you didn't want your friend to come round?

DJ: Yes, I did. I just wanted to be left alone. If I need to do that I'll do it. I didn't want him to have to think for me. You know, I think there's an inability to sort of separate yourself—somehow he makes decisions for me. That could be interpreted as very considerate, but I feel really imposed upon. The way I felt was 'Well, why don't I? Why don't I want to see them about the situation? Am I not concerned that we're in the middle of a crisis?'

LC: Did you have all sorts of mixed feelings then about coming here tonight?

DJ: No, I wanted to come.

LC: We felt it was ever so important to keep the time—to see you.

DJ: No . . . I felt if he had any need to see you it was because he felt inhibited, or wouldn't say what he needed except alone. I don't have the same need.

LC: We respected the fact that you might feel differently—that's why we didn't get in touch.

DJ: Yes, Paul told me you'd said that. But it was peculiar. I started thinking 'Well, why is it that I don't want to get in touch? Is there something wrong? Maybe I don't care?' Again I felt this reaction against Paul seeming to feel that the way I should react is the way he reacts to the situation.

CC: I have the feeling . . . the sort of eruption of anger which occurred last weekend is very close to other feelings as well, which may actually be, at one level, more uncomfortable. When we heard about what had happened we were trying to make sense of it in our own minds in terms of the sequence of your relationship with us.

And we thought together about the weeks we'd been meeting, and some of the struggles we've had to try and get in touch with things that are real.

If you remember, last Tuesday it felt to us that we were getting much more directly in touch with something important when we asked what sessions you felt had come to life—and you mentioned the occasion when you'd come to life over an argument. Life in the marriage seemed to be very much equated with the eruption of anger, and a row, rather than with feelings about closeness. It just made us wonder whether the violent feelings there's so much anxiety about are the crux of the problem, or whether it's more to do with the vulnerability of putting yourselves in each other's hands— putting yourselves in our hands—and having the sort of closeness in which you're very much more exposed than you are with a more calculated distance—where things are kept fairly safe.

. . . we were looking ahead last Tuesday to the meetings we will be having in the weeks to come and the break in the summer. We were also asking about our significance to you, and about your degrees of freedom in the sessions to say what you thought, to differ, and to have things out . . .

LC: With us and with each other.

CC: Yes, and I think also there were some indications that things have changed a little in the weeks since we've been meeting and, para-doxically, we wondered whether that might make things more diffi-cult for you. If you get to the verge of something being better you might be much more vulnerable to the explosive reactions when things are set back. We were talking about the sexual relationship last week—what could be said and what would happen in that con-text.

DJ: That may be, but . . .

CC: That may not be the major reason, but don't dismiss it as one of perhaps many things—perhaps others were more important?

DJ: I was shocked by the way Paul . . . you see, I feel basically we get along alright. I've said this before, that we're fairly compatible; but this made me feel I'd been harbouring some real deception—except that I realise there were tensions and problems. But Paul said the problems are not important if there is an underlying something there—a real relationship, or a closeness, or some compensating factors to hold together; but there is nothing holding it together.

CC: Is that what the shock was about?

DJ: Yes. I just didn't feel that was the case. So that made me feel maybe he has some kind of idea about what he wants and it's impossible for me to provide it, ever.

CC: You have actually, I think, very different perceptions of the meaning of last weekend's row. But having heard what Paul was saying about your feelings in that situation I think you were experiencing rather the same things as him but seeing it from the other end—what can I really offer? What is it that he really wants?—as if you felt demolished.

DJ: Yes . . . you feel like everything disappears.

LC: Did the row really start after that?

DJ: I was trying to remember that. I think so. I think the row started after he said he had to leave.

PJ: No, I said I had to leave after I'd struck you—after we'd exchanged insults and I struck you.

DJ: I don't know. I had the feeling somehow that you were going to go.

PJ: (quietly) no, no, no, no—no, it was afterwards.

LC: I suppose the way I see it more now is that the anger and insults were ways of covering up the helplessness and terrible hurt that was around because of what had been said earlier. You both felt very hurt and rejected.

DJ: You went particularly berserk when I called you a 'whinger'—and I didn't actually expect it to have quite that reaction. He said he wanted me to say what annoyed me . . .

PJ: I called you the name first.

DJ: I never expected him to hit me. All the time I was stunned, but afterwards what annoyed me was that I hadn't just sort of hit him back. I didn't feel particularly hurt or anything; it was like something not happening to you until he picked up the chair—and then I had the vision of what he'd told me about attacking his father and I started to get worried. But he restrained himself.

CC: But it is an indication that the row was charged with more than what was going on in the room—and maybe on both sides. That's where some of the potential lies—to be salvaged by making sense of it retrospectively.

DJ: I don't know. My perception of Paul is that of one long constant moan right at the moment. I thought things were getting better. His perception of the way I react to his insecurity and things is, like, 'pull your socks up', and I don't feel that's my attitude. I have tried to encourage him to do something about the problems but I feel constantly I'm pushed into the role of his mother—like his mother told him: 'you're breathing like that because you want to hurt me', you know?

PJ: It's not so much that I feel you're like my mother. I just feel that you and your family are part of the cold shower brigade. If you've got something wrong, 'take a cold shower, concentrate hard, and with the right spirit it will go away'. Up to a point that's alright but it gets very tiresome and irritating. My problem is that I should have said very forcefully at that point 'Sod off and leave me alone'. But I was remorseful and apologetic and resented that. I know I don't give you enough space. The only thing I can say in my defence after the row was that you appeared to be hysterical and not in control, in a way that frightened me, and I wanted someone to help you.

The crisis of physical separation embodied the catastrophe which Mr and Mrs Johnson felt in their bones would follow from exploring their feelings and opening up to each other. Because they had been unable to 'hold together', it was as if nothing could be taken for granted any longer, and their questions converged into one mass of doubt: perhaps there wasn't much in the relationship? Did they really care for each other? Maybe they couldn't meet each other's needs? Were they very destructive to others? The extract ends with Mr Johnson re-entering the discussion, his contributions reflecting concern for her and their mutual need for space, a theme stressed by his wife earlier in the interview. With that acknowledgement the crisis was weathered, and the following week the Johnsons resumed living together.

From our point of view, the most pressing matter was to ensure that the fabric of the therapeutic container held, and that at least the structured aspect of their relationship with us could be relied upon when everything else appeared uncertain. But we also needed a view of the crisis which would mean something to them and restore a sense of perspective.

What we understood

Momentum around the theme of separation had been building up for some time in the therapy. This first became evident in discussions about the political organisation in which they had met, an organisation which had provided a channel for concerted protest. Although they had withdrawn from membership before starting therapy, the sense of still being vulnerable to the views and criticisms of those they had left behind remained strong during the early period in which we saw them. Indeed, the organisation became a symbol for the kind of institution which demanded corporate uniformity and refused to tolerate individual differences on pain of expulsion. As such it provided a means of discussing the ways differences and partings might be handled by each of them. As with his family, Mr Johnson preferred the clean break, but then felt guilty and the object of criticism, and so became ill, as if this was the price to be paid for autonomy. On the other hand Mrs Johnson was for putting everything in abeyance, so that a mantle of uncertainty was drawn over her allegiances. Yet she had shown her husband the way out of the organisation in the face of much criticism. While her emotional investment in that area had stopped before we met her, Mr Johnson moved from feeling a guilty betrayer to mobilising a self-preserving anger.

The issue of leave-taking also came up prior to a holiday break, eleven weeks into therapy, when the Johnsons were about to visit Mrs Johnson's father abroad. An ordinary task like packing the suitcases exposed the friction between them generated by their uncertainty about who had responsibility for doing what, and how much each could rely upon the other to do things their way. Mr Johnson would either do nothing or would pack up all their belongings very quickly, whereas Mrs Johnson was concerned about an orderly if slower departure. Both said they operated better on their own, especially under pressure, and working together faced them with their different approaches. For Mrs Johnson these were difficult to hold on to without feeling she was manoeuvring her husband into doing something to which he objected; whereas Mr Johnson saw in her face that 'I'd really like to divorce you' look and lapsed into angry inertia.

The visit abroad was not an unqualified success, but it threw into relief the divisive effect Mrs Johnson's attachment to her father was capable of having in the marriage. Mr Johnson felt he had lost his wife during the visit and, coincidentally or not, was ill for most of the trip. His illness prevented Mrs Johnson from spending the time she would have liked with her father and earned her husband only irritable attention. Mr

Johnson referred to 'the most serious row we've ever had' as having taken place on that holiday over their different relationships with his father-in-law. Discussing the incident reinforced his impression that when his wife committed herself to the marriage she had been more concerned with pleasing her father than with pleasing him. To us it seemed that giving up the place reserved for her father was necessary if there was to be room for the marriage to develop. Mrs Johnson needed to part company with her idealised attachment to a dominating parental figure, in the same way that Mr Johnson needed to relinquish his angry attachment to a rejecting and remote parental figure.

Subsequent interviews prior to the crisis centred upon their relationship with each other and their relationship with us. Mr Johnson spoke of his conviction that they ought to be in agreement as a couple. When this wasn't so, differences between them were enlarged out of all proportion, and it felt as if the relationship as a whole came under threat. Mrs Johnson confirmed this assumption by declaring that the reality for her was that relationships *did* break up because of distancing and differences. Her parents' uncompromising attitudes led first to their living oceans apart and then to their divorce. For her, the legacy had been a sense of not belonging.

The absence of a sense of belonging inside themselves, of having a secure place to stand from which to become involved with others, seemed particularly relevant to their fear that expressed differences were destructive and threatened actual separation. We, and they, explored this absence in relation to their absent, or limited, relationships with their same sex parent. Mrs Johnson's alienation from her mother and Mr Johnson's hostility towards his father may have limited their sense of having a secure sexual identity. It left Mrs Johnson fearing that to be a woman meant being walked over, as she believed her mother had been walked over by her father. It left Mr Johnson feeling that to be a man meant having to assert himself violently. The crisis temporarily fused perceptions of the partner with these parental images. Mrs Johnson saw her husband as a 'whinger', a burden, as she felt her mother had been and was determined she should not become herself. Mr Johnson, for a split second, picked up a chair to attack his wife in a way reminiscent of a violent episode with his father.

Both partners had achieved a measure of relief in their families by establishing a better relationship with the parent of the opposite sex than with their same sex parent, and, indeed, than either set of parents had achieved in their marriage. The relief was tempered by the uncertain knowledge that neither could really displace their repudiated parent; were they to succeed, the experience would be frightening because it would unleash the fear of there being no controls in the family. Their shared conflict was of an oedipal nature.

As they began to risk more with each other, their relationship with us began to move. At the outset Mr and Mrs Johnson had behaved as if we were setting an exam which they had to pass in order to be offered, and to be sustained in therapy. They, and particularly Mr Johnson, accommodated us by being 'good clients'.

Even when our expectations were less clear to them, a presumption continued that *we* were defining the relationship and *their* role was to comply. As Mr Johnson concluded in baffled desperation, 'the rules are that there are no rules.' They sought to reduce differences between us and them. We had the sense that no distinctions were made between the two of us, and we found ourselves behaving as if we understood and agreed with each other all the time. Yet we were also afraid that while our pronouncements were heard and received with assent, they were not really registered or taken in.

This situation changed as the therapy gathered momentum, but changed very slowly. Generally speaking it would be as a result of *our* invitations that we would be questioned, as when we asked them whether we had passed *their* exam in terms of their expectations of us. Throughout, we felt we were being preserved from their criticisms by their acknowledging only a low level of expectations, which we could not then disappoint. Yet we thought we became more real to them as people—and also more available to their projections. Mrs Cudmore was perceived as warm and responsive in the sessions, and Mr Johnson valued this, but also felt under attack by her if she made a straight comment. Mr Clulow was perceived as being detached and this was sometimes seen as a lack of concern for them. Whatever we felt personally about these observations, (and however much we hastened to understand them as attributions!) a distinction had been drawn between us, and our relationship had become partially available to be used in the therapy.

Yet the significance of the breaks in their relationship with us was denied, or not responded to when we drew attention to the fact that one or both of us would not be available for them on certain dates. It so happened that during the session preceding the weekend crisis we had told them the weeks we would be away because of summer holidays. We gave them only four weeks notice. The significance of this break following a time when they had been exceptionally angry with each other in the interview, was played down. Mr Johnson assured us he had to be away for one of these weeks anyway, and Mrs Johnson appeared to be relieved by the prospect of some time for them to test each other out without our help. She did add, in jest, that she thought they ought to take our tape-recorder home while we were away. It was four days later that the weekend blow-up occurred.

What we did

The interview transcript following the weekend of their separation illustrates our dual mode of operation; we acted and we interpreted.

Our actions were directed towards maintaining the 'safe house' of therapy which both partners could continue to use despite being blown apart by the eruption between them. We made it clear that their appointments remained unaltered and we expected both of them to attend. At the same time it was extremely important to treat them differently: to allow Mr Johnson the extra session that he requested on his own, and not to insist on Mrs Johnson having to do the same.

In terms of interpretation, we operated in four areas. First, despite the shock of the weekend's events, we attempted to reframe the incident from one which, on the face of it, appeared to be a total disaster to one which held potential. The concrete act of separation was interpreted in the context of their wholly legitimate need to negotiate more space for themselves and each other in the marriage. Second, we interpreted their anger both as an expression of hurt and a means of restoring their distance. We suggested their greater involvement with each other and with us represented a potentially frightening change from which they were tempted to seek refuge amongst a familiar distance and denial of need or attachment. Third, we attempted to contain the impact of the assault by placing the incident in a wider familial context where it might become more understandable and manageable as an example of what might be called 'mistaken identities'. Finally, we drew attention to our part in the incident, having given them notice of a break in therapy at a time when they had been risking more with each other and when they were stressed by external pressures.

Waving not Drowning

The following months of therapy covered little new ground, but allowed for a working and reworking of, by then, familiar themes. The difference between this period and the preceding period lay in the note of optimism which sounded beneath the frequent surges of feeling generated by a mixture of external pressures and personal uncertainty. Although this was a period when we provided an imperfect framework to support the

Johnsons in their endeavour to keep the marriage afloat, it was also one in which, as individuals and as a partnership, they found they would not sink under their pressures but swim.

Following the six-week break for summer holidays there were some difficulties re-engaging with each other. Mrs Johnson said she felt as if there had been no break in the sessions, but found herself wondering, as she had at the outset, how to begin. For us the break had seemed a long one, and we still felt a hidden reproach for taking our leave so soon after a significant crisis in their relationship and at a time when we had become important to them.

As they talked about their marriage, Mr and Mrs Johnson dwelt on some of the differences between them. These tended still to be represented in a polarised fashion, leaving little middle ground on which they might communicate. Mr Johnson talked about the extremes in his reactions to people who were close to him; he either loved them or hated them. Mrs Johnson described him as a person who was 'extremely extreme', whereas she described herself as someone who was 'extremely unextreme'. Our view was that these extremes constituted a means of managing their ambivalent feelings. To take a family example, Mr Johnson felt on firmer ground when he disparaged his father than when he allowed himself to think how his efforts to succeed might be linked with earning father's approval. Mrs Johnson could luxuriate in the benign relationship with her father while he was thousands of miles away and she could divert the irritation she felt with men who could be controlling and intrusive in her life. Together they represented the mixture of love and hate stirred up by important relationships; between them they contained the essential ambivalence which characterised their respective attachments, an ambivalence which was harder for each to manage on their own.

By now it will be apparent that we listened to what they said with an ear to their relationship with us. How would they manage their ambivalent feelings about the commitment to therapy? At a practical level, and having declared that the summer break was not of great significance to her, Mrs Johnson started a course relevant to her professional career, the time of which coincided with their evening appointments with us. In looking for alternative times, we had to settle (because of our commitments) for an arrangement which allowed us to meet only three weeks in every four. Although the effect was therefore to reduce the frequency of their involvement with us, this might also be seen as a welcome sign that Mrs Johnson could claim time for herself and not become trapped in an arrangement because she felt she had no right to question it. The right to question was referred to at a later interview when she remarked on the fact that they never used our names (although we addressed them as Paul and Diana); she said this was because they tended to see us as authority figures. It may be a mark of progress that we became Lynne and Chris before they left us.

Perhaps our failure to provide them with an entirely satisfactory alternative appointment went some way to remove us from the safe pedestal reserved for those quasi-parental figures who needed protection from criticism and attack. But their difficulty in taking us on was replicated in our difficulty in taking them on. There were occasions when we felt the material of the sessions was as much to do with us as with the person or persons who featured in their account, yet we missed opportunities to use these connections and thereby colluded with excluding from discussion some aspects of our relationship with them. This was puzzling, not least because we had resolved from the early stages of therapy to pay as much attention as possible to what was taking place between the Johnsons and ourselves in the sessions. This shared experience, we had reasoned, would mean more than the interesting but perhaps digressive excursions into family histories. We wondered whether our inhibition reflected that of the Johnsons in their reluctance to intrude upon each other. Some confirmation of this was offered at the follow-up interview when we discussed the issue with them. Mrs Johnson recalled saying she had been inhibited by her previous therapist 'drawing parallels with everything,' but had then wondered whether she had inhibited us by saying so.

From what were we and they protecting each other? Did our response complement their endeavour to keep us at bay lest we became the object of their anger with parents who had been so important but then frustrated their needs and wishes? Were we picking up their fears associated with more intimate feelings, reflecting their anxieties about the implications of closeness? If the Johnsons had allowed us to become too important they would not only have risked experiencing the frustration of their needs, with whatever feelings that might evoke, but would have exposed themselves to the vulnerable position of acknowledging their dependence. In phantasy, they may have feared that this would drive them into becoming over-embroiled with us, raising the possibility that they would never be free to leave us.

In this sense we became aware of ourselves as an embodiment of 'the organisation' which had repeatedly been referred to in our discussions. The organisation was described as an aspect of their common past which held them together yet which they wished to shake off. Part of that commonality may have been their own wish to envelop or be enveloped: a wish attributed instead to the organisation. Its attraction was that it represented a cause larger than either of them. In that same characteristic lay the seeds of alienation. Commitment to the organisation made each feel as if they had to surrender their autonomy and identity; it became for them an oppressive social environment. Whether as a positive institution which enabled them to step outside themselves, or as a negative institution about which they could complain, the organisation served to hold them together. 'If we come to a block, the organisation can always be guaranteed to get us communicating,' said Mrs Johnson, and we thought about our role in their marriage. We wondered whether the price of leaving the organisation, of leaving home, of leaving therapy, was the same: no-one would let you go without inflicting humiliation or extracting a tribute of guilt.

Our understanding of the Johnsons led us to believe that the problem of leaving without destroying or being destroyed would be an important preoccupation. This was confirmed by events. In the closing phase of therapy Mrs Johnson secured a senior post with another firm. Leaving her former employer proved difficult. 'I've been made to feel as if I'm breaking off an engagement,' she said, and was concerned that her boss would not manage. Our view was that she dealt with her own sense of loss and anxiety about being hurt by others by making the work attachment seem a one-sided affair. By not acknowledging her own attachment, it only remained for her to extricate herself from the attachments of others, and her only anxiety was about hurting them. Mr Johnson also talked about the experience of separating through the event of his brother's emigration, noting the 'hysterical' reactions of his family at the farewell party. At one time, he said, he would have been an integral part of the family affray, but he described feeling closely identified with his brother, as if he, too, were separate and separating from his family. 'Breaking the habits of a lifetime' was how he described the process of removing himself from the emotional climate and fixed roles of home which had seemed so unchanging and unchangeable to him, and which had so heavily influenced his life. There was a sadness about giving up this past and his part in it, and also about not being able to give it up completely and having to accept it as an unchangeable part of his life experience.

Were they talking about leaving us? When we asked this question directly we received no confirmation either way. Distance was preserved by Mr Johnson describing the therapeutic sessions as containing the 'anonymity of the confessional.' Mrs Johnson referred to the changes and pressures they were under at the time, and their need for therapy as a kind of insurance policy. We thought there was more to it than that. In several of the sessions they talked about their catering arrangements at home—who would shop and who would cook; one source of friction was that each hoped to be catered for by the other but made this more difficult by catering for themselves. We, too, had the feeling that, at times, the 'food' we offered was left, that we were disregarded for fear of becoming embroiled in a relationship which might be hard to leave.

At the same time there was evidence of change. They each felt more confident about themselves and about the marriage. True, there were still arguments, they were under pressure in their work and social lives, sex remained an extremely touchy area of their relationship, but they were talking together about these things, and talking at home outside the confines of the sessions. Mrs Johnson described resisting the temptation to step into the firing line when Mr Johnson was troubled. Mr Johnson talked of the relief of being allowed (allowing himself) to go for a long walk when the pressure to go on the offensive against his wife threatened to prove too much. Each felt less victimised and more confident of finding personal solutions to the pressures of life, and the IMS was associated with the quest for these personal solutions. Increasingly we began to wonder whether they might be dredging for problems in order to qualify for their weekly appointments. When Mrs Johnson arrived late for their last appointment before Christmas, explaining she had taken the wrong exit from the local Tube station and got lost, we thought the end was not far off.

Back to Shore

When the Johnsons returned after Christmas, Mrs Johnson opened by saying they wanted to discuss whether or not to continue coming for therapy. She said they felt more secure together, were handling themselves and each other better, and they were able to talk. This last point was particularly important to her because lack of communication had been a major factor bringing them into therapy. We asked when they were thinking of ending and were told they had that same day in mind.

There is a convention amongst dynamically orientated therapists which frowns upon abrupt endings and stresses the importance of ending well. 'Ending well', in conventional terms, implies giving sufficient notice of the ending date for work to be done on the process of leaving, allowing for some assessment and consolidation of what has gone before, and sufficiently resolving transference issues so that what has been gained is felt to belong to the patient and not to the therapist—who might otherwise appear to retain the secret of life in a locked tin trunk kept under the analytic couch. 'Sufficient notice' is capable of liberal interpretation. An ending date can be set before therapy begins, and some therapists would describe the entire therapeutic process as one of coming to terms with limitations and endings. Our view was that good therapy is like good parenting; its object is to enable people to take responsibility for themselves and develop a secure sense of autonomy so that they can leave therapy. That involves negotiation about ending as much as about other issues.

As we have seen, the issue of 'leaving home', whether 'home' was the Johnsons' residual dysfunctional attachments to parents, the organisation which had absorbed so much of their energy, a previous employer, or therapy itself, had featured in many of the discussions over the preceding months and, in that respect, the suggestion that we should cease meeting was less abrupt and less surprising than it might otherwise have seemed. Thus forewarned, and because we felt it important from our understanding of their experience both that we should not become prohibitive therapists and that they should instigate the ending, we were ready to accept their suggestion. Like family, however, we could not help having some qualms. For our own satisfaction, and we hoped for theirs too, we looked for evidence in the last session to support their decision.

In the first place, both they and we knew that previous holiday breaks had been unsettled periods in their lives, and we wondered how the Christmas holiday had been for them. We discovered they had been using the holiday period as a kind of litmus paper, 'part of the test', to establish whether the time was right to leave us. Both said Christmas had been relaxing and enjoyable, and while they were aware that the holiday period had naturally removed some pressures they, and we, took this as a favourable sign.

Secondly, we wondered whether there had been improvements in the problem areas defined when they first came. We knew from their doctor that both partners, and particularly Mr Johnson, had been frequent visitors at the surgery prior to therapy. We were told by them at this last session (and this was later confirmed by their doctor) that they had not been back to the surgery since they started therapy.

All right, we thought, but perhaps we have simply substituted the IMS for the doctor's surgery. What about the sexual problem which initially brought them for help? Here, the area of improvement was less clear. They were having sex, and they had acknowledged the interpersonal factors which were contributing to the anxiety and lack of spontaneity that was still experienced. Yet each worried that the other was not getting enough out of sex, thinking more about their partner's enjoyment than their own in a way which sustained their inhibitions.

This led us to the problem which we and they had jointly defined as the focus of-therapeutic work: the 'dance routine' which entangled each with the other, left little space for asserting themselves as individuals and which disallowed a sense of separateness in the marriage. In this area there had been some change. Mr Johnson commented that 'at least I can go for a walk without Diana taking it personally now'. He felt less need to run his wife's life, and he thought she allowed him more room to be annoyed and angry. Mrs Johnson, likewise, felt she could express more of herself, and her confidence in her husband reacting less violently than before had increased. Each was more aware of what they were feeling and this allowed them to check out the emotional temperature and, if necessary, control it before a crisis became inevitable. Gaining some understanding of what happened between them had helped Mrs Johnson to feel less confined and more in control of herself, allowing her to risk a little more of herself in the relationship.

The freedom to communicate, they said, had come partly from losing the conviction that each had to provide a solution to the other's moods or problems. Mr Johnson said he had been brought up to believe that life was a series of tests, 'an obstacle race', and he had to pass them all to succeed. He was prone to feeling responsible for every shade of his wife's feelings and troubles, and prone also to reacting angrily when he failed to provide a remedy for them. Now, he thought, he was under less pressure to come up with a solution when they talked, and attributed that to the experience of therapy: 'at the end of the hour we hadn't solved the problem, but it didn't matter'.

Thirdly, in their other relationships there were signs of change. Mrs Johnson had asserted herself successfully in her career and Mr Johnson had detached himself a little from the consuming passions of his family. This was particularly true with regard to his mother. He found he could let things go when she provoked him, and it was even safe enough to tease his wife when his mother came out with characteristically outrageous comments about her cooking. Moreover, he could say things about his father-in-law without upsetting her as much as before.

There was also some movement in their relationship with us. They could tell us they had been frustrated by our detachment—'it was difficult to argue when there was no opponent'—and responsive to our subjectivity (especially when one or other had similar feelings!) At first Mrs Cudmore was seen as the subjective one who might inflame passions and argument; Mr Clulow was seen as the objective one who held out on them. We were intrigued by how similar these perceptions were to the complaints each had made about the other at the start of therapy: Mrs Johnson detaching herself from her husband while he expressed sufficient feeling for both of them. At the last session their perceptions of us had shifted, allowing Mr Clulow to be credited with warmth and Mrs Cudmore with objectivity.

Finally, the crisis of separation had marked a turning point for each of them which allowed the 'problem' to be acknowledged as marital, rather than as an expression of Mr Johnson's personal emotional difficulties. Mr Johnson said that before the incident he felt he was going crazy because his wife would not acknowledge her part in the problem. When she said the marriage was all right he felt his different experience was a kind of madness. Mrs Johnson thought the crisis had enabled her to recognise her own detachment in the face of emotional stress and her part in her husband's desperation. She had not been able to understand why the crisis had seemed unreal to her; her friends had thought the marriage had finally ended and saw her cool reactions as most peculiar. Now, having negotiated a shared problem, some element of blame had been removed, preparing the ground for managing future stressful incidents more openly together.

While these were grounds for feeling confident about ending, they were not necessarily grounds for ending so abruptly. Although endings had been in the air for some time before the final session, the cues had not, perhaps, been made explicit or taken up sufficiently by either side. This suggested that inhibitions in the therapeutic relationship remained strong, that it had not felt safe to express mixed feelings about therapy—their disappointments about what had not been achieved as well as their satisfactions with what had been achieved. The crucial issue of surviving a difference of view about the date of ending was not put to the test and may have cost us a valuable opportunity of working directly with the area of separation and ending which we knew to be important for each of them through what they had told us. Moreover, we failed to explore whether the abruptness of their withdrawal from therapy was a response to our developing importance to them. Perhaps, we wondered, we had surrendered our side of the negotiation about ending thereby replicating an aspect of their problem in the therapeutic relationship?

At the beginning, Mr Johnson had been the one to press for marital therapy while Mrs Johnson had been cautious about coming. At the final session the roles were reversed: Mr Johnson took the lead in saying farewell, while Mrs Johnson added '. . . and we'll probably see you again'.

CHAPTER 6

And After?

The Problem of Assessing Outcome

For most therapies the final treatment session is the last contact between client and therapist. Some consideration may be given in that interview to what has been achieved as a result of therapy, as it was with Mr and Mrs Johnson, but evaluations of this kind are more for the benefit of the direct participants in the therapeutic relationship than for other practitioners, or for the systematic building up of knowledge. Assessing what kinds of change were produced in what kinds of problems, how sustained they were, and what part the therapists and their techniques played in the process, are areas which often remain unexplored. This is understandable in view of the kind of phenomenon under investigation and the complexity of the task.

Perhaps because of the complicated nature of the issues involved, outcome studies have not been popular avenues of enquiry in the field of marital therapy any more than in individual psychotherapy. Moreover, results that are available have sometimes been sufficiently enigmatic to frustrate, if not discourage, ardent practitioners. Back in 1952, Eysenck[1] suggested that approximately two-thirds of neurotic patients in and out of psychotherapy improved, no matter how they were treated or whether they were treated at all. In his review he focused solely on symptomatic disturbances, recognising no other. While these conclusions opened rather than terminated a debate which continues (and now it is held that most forms of psychotherapy are effective with non-psychotic patients[2]) there remains scant information about what works best for whom and why.

Some broad conclusions have been drawn from more recent research into marital psychotherapy. For example, conjoint and group therapy for couples is believed to be more effective than working with partners separately; the efficacy of co-therapy has yet to be established in outcome terms (though when two therapists are employed the quality of their working relationship has been found to be an active ingredient contributing towards success or failure); most positive results from open-ended therapy are said to be achieved in the first five months of treatment; an alliance between clients and therapists is consistently identified as a key factor heightening the treatment effect; and where therapy has an adverse effect, factors associated with the therapists, and their relationship with their clients, have been found to be of greater significance than the psychopathology of the clients.[3] Conclusions of this general nature sometimes conform to and sometimes conflict with the experience of therapists. They do raise two very important questions: What do we mean by success or failure in marital therapy? How is this to be measured?

The Meaning of Success

Popularly, marital therapy is supposed successful if it results in a couple staying together; a decision to separate is equated with failure. The values which individuals (including clients and therapists) hold dear may lead them to regard the breakup of marriage as a regrettable event, particularly when children are involved. The distress in facing a parting of the ways may be harder to bear (for couples and therapists alike) than the sometimes irritating tedium of carrying on with things as they are. And, indeed, accepting the irritating tedium may be a sign of health insofar as it demonstrates coming to terms with what is unchangeable in a relationship.

Other values make the issue less straightforward. The premium placed upon freedom of choice, egalitarianism between men and women, personal autonomy, and accountability primarily to oneself (as distinct from accountability to partner, community, church or state) require more subtle indicators of improvement. For a couple to choose to stay together knowing there are alternatives endows their relationship with a different quality to one in which there is felt to be no escape. Insofar as marriage creates a prison, or encourages a 'taken for granted' attitude, it may diminish the individuals concerned and stifle their potential in all areas of life. Choosing to dissolve a marriage, having come to terms with the implications of this action, may enable couples to accept responsibilities which might otherwise be evaded, and may even facilitate the recovery of mutual liking and respect. The civilising effects of conciliation in divorce proceedings provide evidence that at least one branch of marital work does not require success to be equated with reconciliation.

Success might reasonably be associated with the disappearance of a symptom or complaint presented by a couple as their reason for embarking upon a course of therapy. If a couple delineate a sexual problem in their request for help, as did Mr and Mrs Johnson, an improvement in sexual functioning in the course of therapy might properly be regarded as a successful outcome. Therapies which concentrate upon the symptom alone, and have specific and replicable techniques relatively unaffected by the personality or style of the therapist, are more frequently researched because of the relative straightforwardness of the task. A discrete symptom is treated by a well-defined and repeatable technique, and the results compared with the same symptoms manifest in other patients who are not treated. An improvement in the treated group provides evidence of the efficacy of treatment.

Such an approach necessarily excludes from consideration aspects of the physical, psychological and social environment in which the patient exists and with which he interacts. The effects of these may influence outcome but they will not be taken into account. Nor will account be taken of the latent purpose of presenting symptoms, for example, their function in a relationship and their value as a means of communication.[4] Symptoms are, by definition, the visible manifestation of something larger than themselves, such as an underlying illness or psychological conflict. Symptomatic remission is not necessarily the same as cure. An improvement in one part of the body, one aspect of a relationship, or in one part of a family, may simply divert the manifestation of stress and lead to deterioration elsewhere. This process can work in reverse. Psychodynamic therapists commonly refer to improvements in their clients as flights into health, when describing situations in which the need for further help apparently evaporates at the point the therapists believed they were on to something important or about to face a crunch issue in the therapy. The essential point is that symptoms do not exist as static, isolated entities, patiently waiting to be treated and to have their responses measured. They are part of complex physical, psychological and social organisms which infinitely complicate attempts to run controlled experiments. Researchers may combat this complexity with ever more refined methodologies. The danger is then that methodology is accorded primacy over the subject matter it deals with.[5] The consequence of this has been described in a particularly apt way for marital researchers: 'in science as in love a concentration on technique is quite likely to lead to impotence.'[6]

Any list of symptoms needs to be accompanied by an explanatory hypothesis. For the psychodynamically oriented therapist this involves the assumption that presenting complaints are the product of emotional conflicts. Success will be linked with the reduction of underlying conflicts, personal and interpersonal, which, in turn, has to be shown to render individuals less vulnerable to external stresses and less susceptible to symptom-formation as a means of managing those conflicts.[7] A successful outcome will require the relationship between two individuals (if it continues) to be healthier and more robust after treatment than before. In turn this will require each of the partners to manage their conflicts more constructively than before. These are more exacting criteria of change than remission of a symptom. They reflect the working assumptions of the therapist. In that sense, research into therapy is research into the mind of the therapist.[8]

The Measurement of Change

The main criticisms which are likely to be levelled at this approach are that it is based on theory which is unvalidated in traditional scientific terms and, in particular, that it is too subjective. The first criticism raises an important question about the adequacy of traditional methods of scientific enquiry to the task of assessing change in people and their relationships. Families, marriages and individuals are dynamic organisms constantly interacting with their environment, a highly complex environment which itself is changing and does not readily submit to classical methods of scientific research. Because the factors considered to be of most importance are not easily quantified, research methods cannot rely upon statistical analysis. Because of the impossibility of ensuring controlled conditions comparative studies are fraught with difficulties. Because states of health and illness are relative and context-related there are no simple yardsticks by which improvement or deterioration can be measured. A scientific method suitable for research in the restricted physical sciences (where laboratory conditions can ensure constancy in all the variables relevant to the investigation) is not necessarily suited to the unrestricted sciences.[9] Ironically, it is in the higher realms of the physical sciences, where classical methods of scientific enquiry originated, that the first steps have been taken to review and broaden scientific principles to take account of increasingly complex phenomena.[10]

For all that, it must at the very least be accepted that, to be of use, explanations should have predictive value. The therapist/researcher must be as explicit as possible about his explanatory hypothesis, and he must ensure that the hypothesis is formulated before conducting the follow-up interview. These stipulations at least allow working assumptions which have informed practice to be tested on their own terms, and provide some safeguard against manipulating theory or facts into supporting each other. To reduce the element of subjectivity there is an argument for ensuring that the therapist is not the person who draws up the list of symptoms, formulates the hypothesis, and conducts the follow-up interview.

This last point introduces a dilemma. Objectivity in outcome research may require a distinction to be drawn between research and therapeutic roles. Therapists are likely to look for evidence which supports the usefulness of their work, and overlook evidence which questions or contradicts it. On the other hand, the therapist is in a good position, because of his knowledge of the client, to know which of various subtly different hypotheses speaks most adequately to the client's position, and what limitations it has. The explanatory hypothesis reflects the therapist's perspective, and this cannot be dispensed with when deciding upon outcome criteria.

One of the opportunities created by therapists conducting their own follow-up interviews is the inevitability that the therapeutic relationship will be resurrected in the process. Since the therapeutic relationship is considered by psychodynamic therapists to be the instrument of change, its omission in the follow-up would be serious indeed. Transference and countertransference phenomena are likely to be rejuvenated when therapist and client meet. Comparisons are then possible, in terms of the nature and intensity of these phenomena, between the period during which therapy took place and the time of follow-up.

Transference and countertransference factors will also affect interviews conducted by researchers who have had no previous contact with clients. Among the reasons motivating people to talk about a time in their lives which was, and might still be distressing will be goodwill resulting from the achievements of therapy, disappointment associated with what was not achieved, and perhaps hope about what might still be achieved. Their presence and significance, however, will be harder for the newcomer to detect and understand than for the therapist who has a shared history of experience upon which to draw. The problems of bias in consumer comments are familiar to researchers and touch upon transferential issues. The tendency to report experiences in a way which will justify investments made, or according to what is thought likely to please therapists, has been called the 'hello-goodbye' effect.[11] The skewing may just as well be negative: a predisposition to see the worst in everything, an unresolved transference, or a blazing row immediately preceding the follow-up interview will also influence what is said to the researcher.[12]

It is the process of follow-up, and its links with the process of therapy, which may be overlooked by the non-therapist researcher. Both therapy and research constitute a process of enquiry. By asking questions people are directed towards aspects of themselves and their relationships which they may not previously have considered. The effect may be therapeutic; it may result in change. The therapist/researcher's presence will then have altered the object of enquiry. The deeper the enquiry, the more likely that assessments will change. Results may indicate no more than the point at which investigations cease. A failure to recognise this may result in a segmented representation of reality.

However, there are problems for therapists conducting their own follow-up interviews. In the new context in which they meet their clients are they primarily therapists or researchers? What of the ethical issues connected with inviting people to review a distressing period in their lives, and the responsibilities which follow? Conducting the follow-up interview with the Johnsons and then sharing with them our version of the outcome was, for all of us, the most difficult and least satisfactory aspect of this participatory exercise. It did not end with this account of their follow-up. Despite the familiarity of the issues and our conviction about the gains they had made in therapy we felt as if we had hit them with a powerful condensed interpretation (the explanatory hypothesis) and 'failed' them in our assessment of their performance (follow-up constituting a kind of 'exam'). It was as if *we* were insisting upon one hundred per cent improvement while *their* strength was knowing the limits of change. Some of our difficulties might have been avoided had we been more alive to the issues and adept at handling the situation; others may be intrinsic to the process.

Criteria for an Evaluation

Mr and Mrs Johnson were seen by us for a follow-up interview eighteen months after their treatment ended. Three procedures were used in establishing the outcome criteria. The first was to list the complaints and symptoms specified by the Johnsons and their referrer in letters, application forms, and the initial consultation. From the referrer we learned of a sexual problem which evidenced itself in a *loss of libido* for Mrs Johnson and *sexual insecurity, including fear of rejection* for Mr Johnson. Both were described as being '*over-committed in terms of energy*'. In a second letter the referrer described Mr Johnson as being in '*a very weepy, depressed state*' despite saying the marriage was better, and we knew informally that both parties had separately been *frequent attenders at the surgery* over the year preceding their application for therapy.

From the application forms, Mrs Johnson's problem appeared to be *not knowing, in any specific sense, what was wrong between them.* Mr

Johnson, however, listed *bottling up differences, bitter and destructive quarrels,* and his own psychological state, including '*unaccountable fits of anxiety, crying and sleeplessness*' as his specific problems. We also learned he suffered from asthma and received medication for this. In the initial consultation he defined a cyclical pattern consisting of *involvement with each other leading to a destructive interaction resolved by means of cutting off from each other.* Mrs Johnson described *not being able to activate things in the relationship, sexually and in other ways* as being a problem for her. Although these complaints were enlarged and elaborated upon in subsequent treatment interviews, they contain the essence of what was initially complained about and so constitute a symptomatic assessment.

The next step was to formulate an explanatory hypothesis for these symptoms. This had to take account of the marriage as an entity, as well as its effects on the predispositions of each spouse. Moreover, the hypothesis needed to be brief and intelligible. This aspect of Malan's assessment procedure (see note 7) has drawn criticism from inside psychoanalytic circles because it appears to present a superficial picture, ignoring the complicated workings of psychic mechanisms and the complexity of inner causal factors. At the same time it is an exercise which concentrates the mind wonderfully by, in effect, asking which interpretation the therapists would choose to make given only one opportunity.

The hypothesis was arrived at from the diagnostic assessment and theoretical formulation described in Chapters Three and Four. It ran as follows:

1 Each partner craved satisfaction for unmet emotional needs.

2 Experience had taught them it was dangerous to express their needs because others could not cope and might leave (as in Mrs Johnson's case) or exploit their advantage in the face of what would be seen as weakness (as in Mr Johnson's case.)

3 Frustration of need generated powerful negative feelings which were either denied (Mrs Johnson) or turned in on the self (Mr Johnson) for fear they would endanger the future viability of relationships in general and the marriage in particular.

4 Needs, and the feelings associated with frustration of need, were defended against in a way which presented Mr Johnson, and not the marriage, as the patient. This suited:

a)   Mrs Johnson's tendency to deal with her own needs and feelings by denial (loss of libido) and projection (relating to them in Mr Johnson);

b)   Mr Johnson's wish to qualify for attention yet his need to keep people at bay: they would relate to his performance or symptoms but not to him;

c)   their joint desire to maintain the marriage and their shared phantasy that it would not survive the kind of separateness which permitted each to know about and express their different feelings and needs (the mutually protective function of Mrs Johnson's sexual inhibition and Mr Johnson's symptomatic collapse).

5   The marital system served to keep them in touch with their needs but operated a cut-off mechanism if they came too close. This was because needs and feelings were experienced as overwhelming and capable of resulting in uncontrollable anger and, ultimately, separation if checked or frustrated. Communication between them on an emotional plane was therefore restricted.

The third stage was to identify criteria for improvement. At its most exacting there would be an expectation that all the *complaints and symptoms referred to by the couple and their referrer should no longer exist*. There should be an *improvement in the sexual relationship, with both partners able to assert themselves and lay claim to their own needs as well as responding to those of their spouse.* It should be possible for them to *know about, acknowledge and manage areas of tension in the marriage without destructive rows, cutting off from each other and the formation of various physical and psychological symptoms.* There should be *no obsessional traits, no driven preoccupation with success* and they should have *more energy.* Together they should feel *at ease with their separateness* and *not use acts of psychological and physical separation to communicate anger.* In relation to their therapists they should be *capable of making a balanced appraisal of their experience in therapy,* not feeling constrained by a need either to please or to distance themselves unduly in the follow-up.

If the requirements sound perfectionist, that is what is intended. The criteria provide a yardstick against which actual change can be measured. It would be possible to have a scale of improvements ranging over a number of points, with one end of the scale indicating the best possible change and the other registering deterioration. To achieve these scores with objectivity might require follow-up interviews to be independently assessed by a panel. Marking of this kind was not attempted by us, the purpose of our follow-up being to satisfy our own curiosity as to how they had fared and to illustrate some of the issues raised when attempting to assess outcome.

This model of outcome assessment depends heavily on client and therapist report on which aspects of the therapeutic procedure helped to bring about change. In common with all psychodynamic therapies it is assumed by therapists that the mechanisms for change include developing insight and a capacity for self-awareness, identifying and assimilating previously unfamiliar feelings and behaviour, assuming responsibility for oneself and one's actions so as to break the vicious circles between self and environment that act to inhibit the growth of autonomy; genuine reassurance and direct learning are also tools of the trade.[13] There are also 'non-specific factors'[14] valued by clients such as interest, respect, encouragement, understanding and acceptance—the human qualities—which may have powerful therapeutic effects in their own right. It was our opinion that for the Johnsons the structure and context of our meetings—the safe house which we regularly provided in which risks could be taken and communication encouraged—were also important, perhaps more important than any interpretations we made.

At the final treatment session an informal evaluation of therapy provided some indications of change. There were hopeful signs. Neither partner had consulted their doctor during the course of therapy, and it appeared both were free of physical and psychological symptoms. In other relationships there were signs of self-assertiveness: Mrs Johnson in her career, Mr Johnson with his family. More than this, each was freer than before to talk with directness and humour about the other's family.

In the marriage communication had improved. Some separateness was tolerable. Mr Johnson could go for a walk 'without Diana taking it personally.' Both described an improvement in their confidence in each other. They were more aware of why communication between them had previously been so difficult, especially Mr Johnson, who described having felt responsible for all his wife's moods, and angrily impotent to remedy them. He referred to a direct treatment effect when he equated feeling under less pressure to come up with a solution and his experience of therapy: 'at the end of the hour we hadn't solved the problem, but it didn't matter.' Mrs Johnson had found she could be more open knowing that her husband was less likely to overreact. Consequently, there had been a healthy redistribution of the 'problem' in the marriage, indicating a change in their defensive system. In relation to us there was some evidence of their capacity to appraise the experience of therapy.

Despite these signs of improvement, there had been little change in their sexual relationship. They still lacked spontaneity and assertiveness with each other in this area. Each continued to be more sensitive to their partner's experience than their own, but for reasons to do with personal anxiety rather than mutuality. What remained unclear at the time of their last session was whether or not they were distressed about their sexual relationship. Did their decision to end therapy encourage them to play down their concern in order that we would not resist their departure? Did it reflect a growing hopelessness about our capacity to touch the problem they had first come with? Or were they content to have started the ball rolling between them, confident that they could bring about some improvement without us, given time? We hoped the follow-up interview would shed some light on these questions and provide information about whether changes reported at the end of therapy had been sustained in the intervening eighteen months.

The Follow-Up

Three dimensions of the follow-up interview cast light upon the degree of change which had occurred in the Johnsons' marriage since their first contact with us two and a half years previously: what they said about their present circumstances; what they said about therapy and their relationship with us; what we observed about both. The criteria for change described earlier were examined from these points of reference.

Physical symptoms and emotional state

In terms of their physical condition, Mr and Mrs Johnson were in relatively good health. Mr Johnson was still receiving medication for his asthma, but had suffered fewer bouts of bronchitis than he had earlier in their relationship. Mrs Johnson had been to the doctor because of a rash brought on by the sun, but that was all. She had taken up jogging. Emotional stress had been contained within the marriage. They both looked well. Mr Johnson no longer had a beard and his clean-cut appearance made him look younger and more definite than before. Mrs Johnson was as we remembered her. She was noticeably less convinced about the degree of improvement in herself and the marriage than was her husband.

The sexual relationship

While Mr and Mrs Johnson were having a sexual relationship, and it sometimes worked well for them both, it was unclear as to whether or not there had been substantial change in this area. It might in any case be expected that this would be the last area to change in view of its mutually protective function in the marriage. Their comments reflect a certain tentativeness.

DJ: I find it very painful, I always feel very inadequate about wanting, or needing, or being able to come through in some way . . . It's slightly easier to talk about it because I don't feel so insecure about the relationship as a whole. I think, generally, I do find it hard to express my own needs and desires. It's a general feeling of being out of touch with things, almost of being dead in a way.

Mrs Johnson had remained sufficiently concerned about this area of their relationship to consider whether they ought to consult a sex therapist. Mr Johnson said he was still prone to thinking it was all his fault, but less so than before. He also thought they had enjoyed sex together on occasions, not that this was without its problems:

PJ: The fear for me is that, well, next time we might not be able to repeat this in quite the same way.

Management of tension

There were some differences between Mr and Mrs Johnson about whether discussing together sensitive areas in their marriage helped or not. In connection with sex, Mr Johnson referred to an occasion on which he had felt better once he had talked to his wife about the problem which had occurred between them; Mrs Johnson, on that occasion, had not found relief through discussion.

DJ: I have this tendency to rationalise everything away because I'm afraid of erupting and getting angry about things. It's only when I'm conscious that that's what I'm doing that I can let it out . . . sometimes it's not so smart to let it out, either. There are different ways of dealing with things.

In relation to their respective families there was evidence of an easing of tension. Each felt more confident about saying what they thought to each other in this area, and it seemed that parents were a less dominant preoccupation than they had been when we saw them. Anticipating a future visit to her father, Mrs Johnson said:

DJ: I don't think we'll come to blows in the same way we did on our last trip.

to which Mr Johnson replied:

PJ: I don't feel so threatened by Diana's father.

He recalled that his mistake in the early stages of their relationship had been to woo the acceptance of his father-in-law through compliance, to which his wife replied that once he had discovered how over-committed he had become he had made up by over-reacting in the opposite direction. We witnessed a frank exchange between them about their parents, and were convinced by Mr Johnson's statement that 'the old terror of being transformed into this ten-year-old' had receded. He found he could now say 'no' to his family. On the other hand, tension had been generated between them during a recent visit by Mr Johnson's sister. He had not noticed trouble brewing at this time whereas Mrs Johnson had; she said the problem then became their failure to discuss the incident together.

Tensions resulting from work pressures remained, costing them emotional energy and revealing how ingrained were some obsessional traits, particularly for Mr Johnson. He continued to subject himself to examinations at work, although the only compulsion to do so was his own, in order to satisfy himself that he could do it and to acquire the greater measure of security that additional qualifications brought. He was getting good results but he still felt that less than one hundred percent was tantamount to failure. He described feeling physically sick after his last exam, thinking it was a mistake he had passed. 'I can't take the pressure of exams', he concluded, adding, with more hope, 'I think I'm going to stop taking them'.

Mrs Johnson had changed jobs again since we last saw them. She had felt there was too little for her to do at her previous post. Her present job was demanding and she found herself constantly worrying about not being able to keep up. Mr Johnson had become angry with the way she seemed to invite the persecution of pressure, until he realised that he behaved in exactly the same way.

Surviving separateness

Despite this episode, Mr Johnson believed the most significant change for him had been disengaging himself from his wife in an appropriate way.

PJ: [before] . . . it was rather like poking someone and saying 'go on, you are angry aren't you?' Until in the end not only are they angry but a thousand times more angry than they were.

[now] . . . I find for my part that I wish Diana would sometimes not cut off, but when she does I don't take it so much to heart. I still find the need, sometimes, to feel for her as well as for myself, but I just stop myself doing it—that's her own business and she just has to get on with it beyond a certain point. I'll say something, and if Diana doesn't want to accept it, that's it—I won't pursue it because it's her life.

. . . I don't have to fight her corner as well as my own. I think I used to be like one of those actors who plays two parts. He runs to the other side of the room and says, 'well . . . ', and I used to say 'maybe you think . . . ' or 'maybe this is what you've . . . ' Now I don't; but I fight my own corner. I can't presume to know what you want, but this is what I want. And that's different.

In connection with their feelings about separateness and distance we wondered whether the organisation still featured in their lives. We learned that it did, but to a lesser extent than before. Mrs Johnson was curious to know how large it had loomed in the therapy, adding that she thought it extraordinary that it should still have a hold on them. Mr Johnson recalled that 'you were entitled to mind everyone's business there, and it was unfriendly not to'; to which Mrs Johnson replied 'I didn't know everyone's business—most of it came as a surprise when I found out'. Some of the anger and sense of disillusionment associated with giving up the organisation (which we regarded as one representation of an idealised fused relationship at its best, and a coercive consuming relationship at its worst) was expressed by Mr Johnson in these terms:

PJ: It's not specifically about the organisation, it's about everyone, everything you've believed in in your whole life, and what you thought was right, and just being left outside not being able to know what it's all about—it's the eternal question.

Recalling our hypothesis that therapy and their relationship with us might contain some of the properties of their relationship with the organisation (in terms of how it, and we, were perceived) we wanted to test the extent of change in relation to us.

Appraisal of therapy

The first layer:

PJ: I can only speak for myself, but as far as I'm concerned it seems to me that we have a lot of the same problems but it's just easier to deal with them. It's not that we've changed in terms of personality. . . . For me it had results, and that's all I can say.

DJ: The sessions helped look at things, particularly look at things one wouldn't admit on one's own because it all seemed too threatening. I think we have been able to deal with some situations better.
    I certainly feel we were better off coming. I feel as though we would have come to a . . . probably a bad clash, or something otherwise.

The second layer:

DJ: I felt a little trepidation about coming tonight (*PJ* nods in agreement) because in some ways it is associated with painful things, and that would indicate that they're not resolved completely . . . it made me feel perhaps we should have got it all straight.

PJ: My first reaction, after I put the 'phone down from talking to you was to say 'well, it's like an exam really: I'll only score you say thirty percent? You'll have to do better than that—have to do a resit on that one'.

We asked how they marked us?

PJ: It's very difficult for us to do that because we've nothing to compare you with.

Then what did they remember?

DJ: You're both slightly different. You're (*CC*) slightly cool and objective and Lynne seemed to be more emotional, or reacted—and

I thought that was quite useful actually. It wasn't as if for your job you had to be one thing; there was a useful counterbalance—particularly for me because I find it very difficult to express things and could identify with some of Lynne's responses. Then I wonder why I couldn't have said it. It's a relief when someone else says it and I don't have to be on the line.

(She later referred appreciatively to a television programme in which the therapist had made members of a family speak directly to each other and not through him).

PJ: You (*LC*) got a lot of my antagonism whereas Chris was more laid back. I remember you saying 'do you always have to be told' when I said to Diana how could I know what was going on if she didn't tell me.

The problem for us in assessing what the Johnsons said about therapy was knowing how far we continued to set the conditions by which the relationship would be judged. We thought they remained constrained in what they said. Quite clearly it had been difficult for them to come back to see us, to talk and read about their therapy, and to re-open old wounds. That they managed this might be taken as evidence of their greater resilience; of a feeling that they could not turn us down; or of a hope they might return to us for therapy. Mrs Johnson had not wanted to read the manuscript to begin with, and thought we ought to go ahead and publish without reference to them. Her view changed in the course of the two meetings we had with them and at the end she asked to be sent a copy of the book when it was published. Yet we were left with some discomfort. Would they feel able to tell us if they did not want their experience to be made public? While we asked this question and were reassured by their reply some of our doubts remained.

It is right to end with the incompletely answered question rather than with a declaration of certainty. If there is one cluster of attributes vital to the survival of marital therapists it is the ability to tolerate uncertainty, to expect not to know, and to live with a certain amount of confusion and discomfort. The follow-up interview answered some of our questions and not others. The same might be applied to the experience of therapy for the Johnsons. They had ended, they said, not because all their difficulties had been resolved, but because they had learned sufficient from the therapeutic encounter 'to be able to cope a bit better.'

Notes and References

CHAPTER 1

1 Between 1980 and 1983 the Study Commission on the Family (as it was then known) published a series of monographs about the family as it appeared through the eyes of demographers. Three are particularly relevant to marriage-watchers: Dominian J (1980) *Marriage in Britain 1945–80*; Rimmer L (1981) *Families in Focus; Marriage, Divorce and Family Patterns*; S C F (1983) *Families in the Future*.

2 Charlin A J (1981) *Marriage, Divorce and Remarriage,* Harvard University Press.

3 Clark D and Samphier M (Autumn 1983) 'Public Attitudes to Marital Problems', *Marriage Guidance Journal* 2–8.

4 Popay J, Rimmer L and Rossiter C (1982) *One Parent Families*: *parents, children and public policy,* Study Commission on the Family.

5 This estimate was made by Dr J Dominian at a symposium held in 1983. The greater part of the figure derives from an estimate of unmeasurable costs: hours lost through absenteeism at work owing to marital discord, the cost of psychotropic drugs prescribed to relieve family stress, etc.

6 This distinction was originally drawn by Jessie Bernard in her book *The Future of Marriage*, published in 1976 (Penguin).

7 Clulow C F (1982) *To Have and To Hold. Marriage, the first baby and preparing couples for parenthood,* Aberdeen University Press.

8 Dearnley B Three into two might go. Unpublished paper given at a Day Conference on '*A Natural History of Marriage*', May 1982.

9 The IMS is based in the Tavistock Centre, 120 Belsize Lane, London NW3 5BA. Its first major publication, *Marriage*: *Studies in Emotional Conflict and Growth* (ed Pincus L, 1960) lays the conceptual foundation on which subsequent work has been built.

10 Sutherland J (1979) *The Psychodynamic Image of Man*, Malcolm Millar lecture, Aberdeen University Press.

11 Clulow C *et al.* (1981) 'Facing Both Ways. The role and task of social work', *Social Work Today,* 13, no. 15, 13–15.

12 Mattinson J and Sinclair I (1979) *Mate and Stalemate: working with marital problems in a Social Services Department,* Blackwells, Oxford.

13 Office of Health Economics (1972) *Medicine and Society: The Changing Demand for Medical Care.*

CHAPTER 2

1   This phrase was coined by Douglas Woodhouse of the IMS.
2   The originator of this story is not known. It was first published by the author in 1979 under the title, 'The first baby and stress'. In Wood C (ed) *Health and the Family,* Academic Press.
3   See Cohen N and Pugh G (1984) 'Presentation of marital problems in general practice', *The Practitioner* 228, 651–6.
4   Britton R (1981) 'Re-enactment as an Unwitting Professional Response to Family Dynamics', in Box S (ed) *Psychotherapy with Families,* Routledge and Kegan Paul.
5   Balint M (1964) *The Doctor, His Patient and the Illness,* Pitman Medical.
6   See Woodhouse D L (1977) 'Referral from General Practice to specialised agencies', *Proceedings of the Royal Society of Medicine* 70, 498–502.
7   Reder P and Kramer S (1980) 'Dynamic aspects of professional collaboration in Child Guidance referral', *Journal of Adolescence,* 3, 165–73.
8   Strean H S and Blatt A (1973) 'Some Psychodynamics in Referring a Patient for Psychotherapy', *Psychoanalytic Review* 60, no. 1, 101–10. For the institutional dimensions see also Will D and Baird D (1984) 'An integrated approach to dysfunction in interprofessional systems', *Journal of Family Therapy,* 6, 275–90.
9   Graham H and Sher M (1976) 'Social Work and General Practice: report of a three year attachment', *Journal of Royal College of General Practitioners,* 26, 95–105.
10 Brannen J and Collard J (1982) *Marriages in Trouble: the process of seeking help,* Tavistock.
11 A particularly useful book examining this theme in relation to communities and institutions, as well as people, is Peter Marris's *Loss and Change,* published 1974 by Routledge and Kegan Paul.
12 Clulow C (1976) 'Crossing the Bar: An Exploration of the Feelings and Difficulties Associated with Working at the Point of Referral'. Unpublished paper read at the *Tavistock Clinic Scientific Meeting* TIHR Doc. 2T 56.
13 This approach is advocated in the Home Office/Department of Health and Social Security Consultative Document *Marriage Matters* (1979) HMSO.

CHAPTER 3

1   For a different diagnostic style see the opening of Malan D (1979) *Individual Psychotherapy and the Science of Psychodynamics,* Butterworth.
2   For a discussion of psychodynamic factors which have a bearing on the use of conjoint or separate interviews see Skynner A C R (1969) 'Indications and contra-indications for conjoint family therapy', *Int Jnl Soc Psychiat* 15, 245–9, and (1976) *One Flesh Separate Persons: Principles of family and marital psychotherapy,* Constable. Also Lyons A (1973) 'Therapeutic Intervention in relation to the Institution of Marriage', in Gosling R H (ed) *Support, Innovation and Autonomy,* Tavistock.

CHAPTER 4

1   For a discussion of this concept and its relation to projective identification
    see Jaffe D S (1968) 'The mechanism of projection: its dual role in object
    relations', *Int Jnl Psychoanal,* 49, 662–77.
2   Ogden T H (1982) *Projective Identification and Psychotherapeutic
    Technique,* Jason Aronson, New York.
3   Zinner J and Shapiro R (1972) 'Projective Identification as a Mode of Per-
    ception and Behaviour in Families of Adolescents', *Int Jnl Psychoanal* 53,
    523–30.
4   Willi J (1982) *Couples in Collusion,* Jason Aronson, NY, London.
5   Bannister K and Pincus L (1971) *Shared Phantasy in Marital Problems,*
    Institute of Marital Studies.
6   See Mattinson J (1981) 'Childlessness.' Unpublished paper given to the
    London Medical Group Conference entitled *The Creative Urge,* (February
    1981), and Mattinson J (1984) 'Abortion and Marriage'. Paper given to
    CIBA conference entitled *Abortion: Medical Progress and Social Implica-
    tions* (November 1984). To be published.
7   Daniell D (1984) Love and Work. A consideration of love and work as
    complementary aspects of identity. Paper given to the Rugby Research
    Conference, April 1984. Awaiting publication in the *International Journal of
    Social Economics.*
8   John Bowlby's seminal work on attachment behaviour has been published in
    three volumes under the title *Attachment and Loss,* Vol 1 *Attachment*
    (1969), Vol 2 *Separation Anxiety and Anger* (1975), Vol 3 *Loss, Sadness and
    Depression* (1980), Hogarth/Institute of Psycho-Analysis. For an introduc-
    tion to his ideas see Bowlby J (1979) *The Making and Breaking of
    Affectional Bonds,* Tavistock.
9   For a good summary see Scharff D E (1982) *The Sexual Relationship. An
    object relations view of sex and the family,* Routledge and Kegan Paul.
10 These terms were applied to object-relations theory by Fairbairn. His writing
    is not readily accessible and is best approached through the commentaries of
    others, for example Scharff (see note 9 above) or Guntrip H (1961)
    *Personality Structure and Human Interaction: The Developing Synthesis of
    Psychodynamic Theory,* Hogarth/Institute of Psycho-Analysis.
11 Ezriel H (1951) 'The Psychoanalytic session as an experimental situation', *Br
    Jnl Med Psychol* 24, 30–4.
12 Davis G and O'Farrell V (1976) 'The Logic of the Transference Interpreta-
    tion'. *Int Review of Psychoanal* 3, 55–64.
13 Freud S (1896) Further Remarks on the Neuro-psychoses of Defence (phrase
    first used in this paper; see *Standard Edition* Vol III, p 170).
14 Sutherland J D (1963) 'Object Relations Theory and the Conceptual Model
    of Psychoanalysis', *Br Jnl Med Psychol* 36, 109–24
15 Woodhouse D L (1975) Personal Development and Marital Interaction,
    Marriage Guidance 15, 349–68.
16 See Salzberger-Wittenberg I (1970) *Psychoanalytic Insights and Relation-*

ships. A Kleinian Approach, Routledge and Kegan Paul and Segal H (1964) *An Introduction to the Work of Melanie Klein*, Heinemann Medical.

17 Winnicott D W (1974) *Playing and Reality*, Penguin.

CHAPTER 6

1 Eysenck H J (1952) The effects of psychotherapy: an evaluation. *Jnl Cons Psychol* 16, 319.

2 Glick I D and Kessler D R (1980) *Marital and Family Therapy*, Grune and Stratton.

3 Gurman A S and Kniskern D P (1978) 'Research on marital and family therapy: Progress, perspective and prospect', in Garfield S L and Bergin A E (eds) *Handbook of Psychotherapy and Behaviour Change*, Wiley.

4 Clulow C F (1984) 'Sexual Dysfunction and Interpersonal Stress: the significance of the presenting complaint in seeking and engaging help', *Brit Jnl Med Psychol* 57, 371–80.

5 Williams G (1983) Methodological chauvinism in the philosophy of science, *Brit Jnl Med Psychol* 56, 293–7

6 Berger P L (1966) *Invitation to Sociology: A Humanistic Perspective*, Pelican.

7 For an outline of method see Malan D H *et al.* (1968) A Study of Psychodynamic Changes in Untreated Neurotic Patients I', *Br Jnl Psychiat* 114, no. 310, 525–51.

8 A comment made by Dr Arnon Bentovim at a Tavistock Scientific Meeting considering outcome research (12 November 1984) impressed this point on me.

9 For a discussion of this question see Pantin C F A (1968) *The Relations between the Sciences*, Cambridge University Press.

10 See Capra F (1982) *The Turning Point: Science, Society and the Rising Culture*, Fontana.

11 Paolino T J and McCrady B S (ed) (1978) *Marriage and Marital Therapy: Psychoanalytic, Behavioural and Systems Theory Perspectives*, Brunner/Mazel.

12 Hunt P (1984) 'Responses to marriage counselling', *Br Jnl of Guidance and Counselling* 12, no. 1, 72–83.

13 See Malan D *et al.* (1975) 'Psychodynamic Changes in Untreated Neurotic Patients II—Apparently Genuine Improvements', *Archives Gen. Psychiat*, 32, 110–26.

14 Frank J D (1974) 'Therapeutic Factors in Psychotherapy', *American Jnl of Psychotherapy* 25, 250–61.

Postscript

While this account of a marital therapy represents work undertaken by the Johnsons, Lynne Cudmore and myself, and cannot claim to be typical of therapy offered by the IMS as a whole (as can no one therapy since each is specific to the interpersonal context in which it occurs), nevertheless we worked in the IMS, subject to its procedures, and were very identified with the working philosophy shared by its staff. We owe a debt of gratitude to the Johnsons for allowing us to use their experience of therapy, and to our colleagues for the comments they have made about our account of it. Particular thanks are owed to Paul Pengelly for his detailed editing, and to Margaret Spooner for typing the final manuscript so ably and speedily. Linda Besharat and Maureen Rooney also helped by typing earlier drafts.